Resilience:

Staying Strong Through The Struggles

Sharon Lange

IBSN

978-0-473-66770-2 (Paperback)

978-0-473-66771-9 (Kindle)

Forward

♥

Sharon is a lady on a mission. A mission to prove to herself and readers that resilience is the key to bouncing back, that falling and getting back up makes you stronger.

In this book Sharon uses her lifetime of adverse and positive experiences to help readers better manager their lives. So if you are in a dark space, depressed, suffering anxiety or grief, read on. Sharon has been there, done that, she has proved that we don't need to be stuck in the past, that we can change our lives.

A strong message in this book is the importance of positive relationships, be it friends, family, partners and work colleagues. Also, the need to fit in, feel that you are safe and belong.

One thing that has always fascinated me and I have studied, is how significantly our past can influence our lives, if we allow it. When we hold onto the past we attract and experience patterns of behaviour that we keep repeating, which can be negative or positive. Reading this book shows you that.

So if you need help to move on in your life read on.

Raewyn Weller
Author of Your Health is Your Greatest Wealth

Preface

♥

Trauma is intergenerational. Parents ALWAYS do their best with what they have. Sadly, sometimes what they have is a broken spirit and a heart full of pain. From here, addictions, abuse, dysfunctional relationships and depression are virtually inevitable.

To my mum, I know you always did the best you could, with what you had. I know you hold onto a lot of negative feelings, and you think that I blame you. This is certainly not the case. You were a child raising a child of your own. You had no positive role models to guide you in the right direction. Mum, you taught me many great things, such as having values, manners and beliefs. You had high expectations of me – you were strict, and this has paid off. I know I don't say it often, if ever. But I am proud of you. And I know you can and will heal from your trauma. Thank you for giving up your life at the age of fourteen to raise me, you could have given me up for adoption, and who knows what life I could have ended up having.

For almost ten years now you have been alcohol free. I know you have always worked really hard on your childhood trauma, going to different therapists and I know you have already come a long way. Keep going, keep looking forward and remember, you cannot change the past, it's what you do and how you react today that matters and is important.

Disclaimer

♥

This book is a memoir—reflections on the author's recollections of her childhood. Some events have been compressed, and dialogue has been recreated.

Names and identifying characteristics have been changed to protect the privacy of those involved.

It is understood and acknowledged that reading this book may bring up some strong emotions. This book is intended to share the authors story and offer help to others. If you find yourself feeling like you are struggling or having thoughts of suicide, always consult with a trained professional.

The reference section lists many helpful references including:

Lifeline: 0800 543 354

Youthline: 0800 376 633, or you can text them at 234.

Suicide Crisis Helpline: 0508 828 685

Parent Help: 0800 568 856

Anxiety NZ: 0800 269 4389

Acknowledgments

♥

"*Feel grateful, feel free, feel loved.*"
I am so thankful for all the amazing people who have come into my life over the years. I have had many people influence me in positive ways, challenge and encouraged me. I also want to thank those who have come into my life, be it for a short or long time, who may have exited in a negative way. Every person that has come into my life has come for a reason—to teach me something I have needed to learn. If I haven't personally thanked you, you can see that I would be here forever and I could almost write a book on thanking all those that have or are in my life today. I have amazing people in my life, too many to name. But I am sorry if you didn't get a personal mention. I did think of so many people to thank that I couldn't add as it would just go on and on.

My mum. I would like to thank my mum, who gave up her life at fourteen to have me! I know it could not have been easy—a child bringing up a child. I know she did her best, especially since she has told me she did not have her mother as a positive role model. Thank you for having me, believing in me and doing your best.

I would like to thank my dad and step mum for our conversations over the years, believing in me and being there for me. For never judging me and allowing me to be me. I know I was a troublesome child at times (especially when I lived with you when I was eighteen!), but I have always been grateful for you both. Dad I will always be "your little girl".

To my siblings, I love you so much. We may not see each other often, but when we do, we always have a great reunion – with lots of laughs. Growing up, I always felt responsible for you, and I am proud of who you are today. Keep being you and believing in yourself.

Thank you to my papa. I always remember my papa being the one person I could always rely on. He was my biggest idol in life, my constant, my everything, he was my favourate person in the world. Our love and connection we shared was endless and unconditional. Papa taught me so many things in life, he will always have a special place in my heart. I wish he was still here today to read my book and go through this journey with me, but I know he is close with me every step of the way.

Thank you to my husband, Stu. My rock, who always supports me and all of my crazy ideas, even when he thinks they're crazy. He always stands by me, and I know his love for me in unconditional. Thank you for being there for me, listening to me—pushing pause on the TV every five minutes to listen to me! Thank you for asking to read my chapters and taking an interest in my writing, and at times even helping me with content for my book! I am not sure I would have been able to achieve writing this book without your support. I love you so much, and love everything that we share and do together.

My best friend Tarsh, one my longest friends, since we were four-teen-years-old! You have always been there for me, never judged me, and have put up with me being selfish at times (in our early twenty's). We have both been through so much together, we will always remain best friends and love each other. Thank you for being the amazing person you are, listening to my ideas and just always being there for me. I am so proud of you and will always be there for you too. Love you always, my Tarshy.

My three girls, my rocks, my world, my absolute everything that I live for in life. The one thing in life that I am so proud of, knowing that I have given them a better life then I had—a life they will never understand, a life I certainly never want them to experience. Thank you for your love, support and encouragement. I love you all to the moon and back, and I am so proud of the beautiful young ladies you are. Keep being you and believe in yourselves. Listen to your heart and let it take you where you want to go.

My cousin, Kat, my favourite cousin. We didn't meet till I was about twelve-years old – but I feel like I have known you my whole life. You have never judged me and I have always trusted you 100%. I am so proud of the amazing person you are and the challenges you have overcome. I love you so much. Thank you for being there for me and the fun we had as teenagers!

Thank you to my close friends Pania, Lorelei and Chrissy. You all played a special part in helping me along this journey, and for that I will be forever grateful. Thank you for putting up with my "overthinking moments" and listening to my ideas. I value your opinions, your honesty and your non-judgments.

My friend Willie, you are part of the reason I started writing. You always said to me "you should write a book". And when I asked you "what would I write about?" you told me "Resilience." Thank you for all your support and advise over the years.

A big thank you to the people who I interviewed for my book! Thank you for taking the time to share parts of your story. I am so honoured that you have allowed me to write about you in my book!

Thank you to Iris who helped me with the design of the book cover.

Thank you to Bianca, who designed my cover for the well-being journal and took the photos that are on my cover. I had a lot of fun during the shoot!

I would like to thank Ilana. I recently met Ilana through a book we co-authored together, which didn't end up getting published! That's a story for another day! Thank you for all the Zoom calls, our messages back and forth to each other and helping me with everything. I am so glad our paths have crossed.

Lastly, Raewyn Weller, author of "Your HEALTH is your GREATEST WEALTH", whom I met while camping one year. Thank you for your guidance and support throughout my journey of writing this book.

Contents

♥

1. Introduction   1

2. House 262: Where It All Began   9

3. Is This What It Feels Like to Live in a Family?   17

4. On the Move... Again!   25

5. Not a Family Anymore   33

6. A Big Move to Palmerston North!   35

7. Sixteen Years Old—and PREGNANT!   47

8. Fear From My Mother   52

9. The Breakdown   57

10. Distraction, Maybe?   62

11. Meeting Stu   69

12. She's Coming Home   76

13. Resiliency   80

14. Determination   92

15. What Success Means to Me   102

16. Who Influences You and Why It's Important   112

17. My Influences   116

18. Subconscious and Conscious Mind   122

19. How I Lost My Values   125

20. Overcoming a Storm   131

21. Falling, Hurting and Getting Back Up   135

22. Everyone has a Story!   143

23. Tools that helped me   156

24. Instruction Manual for Life   164

25. Having and Setting Goals   167

26. The Last Chapter   183

27. Conclusion   198

28. Website and Book Recommendations   202

29. Vision I Created   204

Introduction

♥

"Be who you are and be proud of it"

Why I wrote this book:

For most of my adulthood, I have thought about writing a book about my life. Not because I want people to feel sorry for me, or beacuse I am a victim. I want you, the reader, to know that I am a surviver. I am a survivior of unimaginable trauma that took place during my early childhood into my teenage years.

I was affected by trauma, violence, alcohol abuse and my parents separating when I was eleven-years-old. At the age of fouteen, I was placed in foster care, being separated from my siblings.

I didn't know growing up in this environment would have such an impact on me emotionally. For many of my teenage to early adulthood life I tried to pretend these stories didn't exist.

I was longing for the feeling of connection with friends and family. What was it like to live a life that was stable, with a mum and a dad? I just wanted to feel accepted and safe. After growing up, experiencing childhood trauma from as young as I can remember, I felt lost. Who was I? I felt numb. I actually couldn't tell you what emotions I was feeling.

School was a chore. I always struggled to learn. The teachers would always say, "Sharon has the potential to do well, she just needs to apply herself." Well, in all honesty, how could I? All I could think about was wanting to fit in, wanting to feel safe. And I was constantly worrying about what it was going to be like when I got home.

It took many years for me to come to the realisation and accept that I'm a statistic. I've been through many childhood traumatic experiences, and I believe resilience has helped with my survival today.

Fast forward to 2022. I'm forty-one-years old. Three years ago I thought to write a book and felt inspired to share my story – aiming to share with you the tools that have helped me and the things that I have learnt to help me retake control of my life. I'm proud of the person I've become today. I didn't always feel this way. I want to share this journey with you – a story of a confused, young lady, searching for a family, for stability and for love.

I'm sitting her today, thinking and reflecting on my journey of writing this book while staring out the window of my dining room. It's a nice sunny day, but it's cold outside. I think to myself, wow, this book has been over three years in the making! What a great inspiring journey it has been! I have learnt so much more about myself and my family. I've even done some amazing healing along the way! I have grown so much. How privileged I've been to get this far in life. But life has not always been a privilege. I've seen and heard things a young child should not. I've lived in situations that I believe I shouldn't have. And, I have survived.

All those who have crossed paths with me and know me well know that I am a great talker! Most of the time, I'm positive and optimistic, but I have been through some hard times. I have fallen, but I've gotten back up. I hope this book inspires everyone who reads it to know that you too can get through the struggles in your life.

I have a story that I want to share as many of us do, and I hope I can encourage others to believe that you do not have to be a victim in your own life. I read this saying somewhere, "You can be a victor or you can be a victim", and I believe I am the victor! You can be too! Life is hard for many of us, but that does not define who we are as people. Going through hard times and negative experiences I believe helps us to understand people and possibly to even understand ourselved better. I think by going through some experiences, we don't need to judge, and we certainly don't have to pretend to be something we are not.

Don't get me wrong, this took me a long time to realise. For years after meeting my husband, I pretended to be something I wasn't, not just to him but to his family and friends. I was embarrassed of my past, embarrassed that I didn't have anything and that I hadn't achieved anything. I had to learn to quit pretending to be someone I wasn't out of shame for my past and a failure to live up to my own realistic expectations. Stu's family and friends were successful! They had their own homes, were married and some had businesses! I had gorwn up wanting all these things. I imagined my life as a business woman, but with the life I had growing up I thought, how on earth would I ever get this? I knew deep down inside of me that this was the life I wanted for myself, and I was not going to give up unitil I got it. I was determined to find a way to not repeat history – to break the cycle.

Stu has taught me to be proud of my past – the past has helped shape who I am today – and accept how I turned out. Meeting Stu most definitely changed my life for the better. I am forever grateful for his love, encouragment and support.

I am excited and also nervous about this book. A lot of hard work has gone into it, including many days of writing notes and reading through them – almost to the point where I've gotten sick of reading this book! Through all the hours of research I wanted to share with you that not only do I have a traumatic story to share, but others do too. To share their stories I interviewed six people. These people had also been through struggles and traumatic experiences. Often, when we meet someone we have no idea what that person has been through. It's not like you go around with a sign on your back that says "I have had a traumatic life!" And honestly, why would you do that? I wanted to share with you the stories of six of the strongest people I have the honour of knowing.

Everyone has a story. Some stories are so horrible you wonder, how did that person survive? You look up to that person with amazement. But when it's yourself, you don't think you're that special. Well let me tell you, every one of you are special and your stories do matter! No matter what you have or haven't been through in life, you are important. You have a story and YOU MATTER!

Trauma is an interesting subject. It effects each and every one of us differently. Some of us may experience the same or a similar event, however, whether or how we are affected by it or not can differ, and how we're supported afterward and possibly guided through the traumatic experience can also make all the difference. Trauma affects many of us, from children to adults. And it is possible you may have experienced more than one traumatic event in your lifetime. It's important to seek professional help if you've been through any traumatic experience that's affecting your life. You may ask how will I know trauma has affected my life? You may feel overwhelmed with life, stressed all the time, lack of sleep, you may rely on alcohol or drugs to numb the pain, you may feel anxious, sad or you may not even know how you are feeling. These are just some ideas on how you may be feeling any of these that I have suggested or you know your children or you are affected by trauma, I highly recommend seeking professional advice. There are many trauma councillors out there that may be able to help. I have a list at the front and the end of this book of people and groups to phone. If these are not in your area I suggest looking at Google and researching someone you can connect with.

It's important to find a way to feel at peace with your story, accept it for what it is and be the person you want to be. This is journey that only you can go on. I can help you through your journey and offer suggestions and navigation, but ultimately your journey is in your hands. I will go into further detail with ideas that helped me, and that I hope can help you get through the nightmares of your past, so that you can be fully present today. You can be anything you want to be be in life, but first you have to address the emotional patterns that are keeping you stuck. You may not even be aware you are stuck? Or be ready to make those hard changes. Please know you are not alone with this thought, and there is support out there.

I want you to know, this is my perspective on my life. What you are about to read is how I saw it first through my memory of a three-year-old, through my teenage years to now. How my percpective has changed as I view it through my forty-year-old eyes. So those reading my book who may have known me through these years of my life may not have thought or known some of these things to have taken place, or they may have remembered them differently. That's okay, neither is right or wrong. I am writing my story on my perspective.

This book is written with love. Written with the intent of being respectful and thoughtful. I do not blame any of my upbringing on my parents or family – balme, anger or resentment will eat you up. My parents, and their parents also survived struggling upbringings. How were they to know to provide stability, love and predictability to their lives and their children? They were never taught this themselves.

The important thing I want you to know is that I'm sharing my story to show and explain to you how a life of traumatic experiences does not have to define the person I am today, nor does it have to define the person you are or want to be. In fact, I believe the traumatic experiences I endured during my childhood have helped shape the person I am today. And I also hope that you may find comfort in some of or all of the stories and tools that I share.

You are the only one who can control what you do, what you think and feel. If you want things to improve in your life, you have to improve them.

If you want things to get better, you have to take the action to make the changes to improve the things you want improved. And finally, if you want change in your life, yup, you got it - you have to take action to change anything! I can help you on this journey and offer advice, but ultimately, you have to do the work. Firstly, change the way you think! Make the choice to be aware of your thoughts. When you notice negative thoughts appearing, ask yourself, are these thoughts absolutely true? How do you know they are true? And replace every negative thought with a positive one, or something you are grateful for.

During my journey of healing, I tried many different strategies to help myself. At the times there seemed to be nothing that worked. I'll share with you some of those tips and tools that have helped me. I believe it was ultimately time, believing in myself and not giving up, that worked for me. It takes time to improve or change you way of thinking or acting. Be gentle on yourself, and allow yourself the time. It won't happen overnight, but if you continue to work hard you will eventually heal through your journey.

Everyone is different, and I don't expect all the tips and tools to work for all of you. The starting point to improving your life begins with you.

What I recommend you do before you go too far in this book is find yourself a diary, journal or note book where you can write notes and journal your thoughts and feelings. If you come across any quotes along the way that you love, write these down too. Go back to them as often as you need to.

There are also twelve monthly challenges that I recommend you try. I have designed these from what I have found useful. These can be started on any month, and you can put in as much or little effort as you'd like. Ideally, you'll aim to do these challenges everyday. If everyday is not possible, I would recommend a minimum of three days each week for the month, of each challenge. At the end of the month, reflect on how your month went, what you're feeling and what your thoughts are.

I do have a PDF or printed version of these available if you'd like to purchase them. Alternatively, it's easy to create your own. The challenges throughout the book go into more detail.

The twelve-monthly challenges:

- Write down what you are grateful for every day.

- Immerse yourself in nature. Go for a walk, sit with the trees, listen to the sounds you hear.

- Do something kind for someone. Someone you know or don't know.

- Learn. Read or listen to podcasts. Educate yourself with some new information.

- Give yourself permission to say NO. Make a choice everyday to forgive.

- Concentrate on your sleep. Ensure you have a good nights sleep. Bath before bed, meditate.

- Be aware of the food and drink you're putting into your body. If you drink alcohol, you could choose not to drink for a month.

- Do something each day that lights you up. It could be draw, paint, knit, or a hobby you haven't done in a long time.

- Set yourself a SMART goal. See chapter on setting goals for guidance around this.

- Play, have fun, laugh.

- Look at yourself in the mirror – dig deep to who you are, look at your values. There is a values excerise later in the book you could follow.

- Finally. CELEBRATE YOU! You have made it through the twelve monthly challenges.

How are you feeling? What's changed? What hasn't changed? Write these thoughts down. Message me if you want to, I am always here.

I hope you enjoy reading about my journey, my childhood traumatic experiences and the tools that helped me get through some of these struggles.

I hope some of my tools may support you in your journey too, or that just reading my story may give you some inspiration.

Thank you so much for purchasing my book. I am so grateful for all the support. I wish you all the very best, and hope you find some great pleasure in learning more about my story.

Arohanui (Much love to you all)

Sharon

House 262: Where It All Began

♥

"We all have stories—my story has helped shape who I am today and for this I am grateful."

House number 262: A small brick house with French doors off the lounge door. The front door had brown coloured glass. That brown colour reminds me of the '80s. This is the house where my mum and I lived, on a busy road in Auckland. I was just three years old. I have a few memories of this house. I can still remember the front door and my bedroom so vividly. The memories are not good ones though.

What is the earliest memory you have of your childhood? What were you feeling? Is it a loving, positive memory? This may not be the case for all of you. It is suggested that most children under the age of seven do not have memories of that age! That seems so crazy.

This was certainly not the case for me. In this chapter I'm going to share with you a couple of the earliest memories I have from when I was three years old, living at 262, the red brick house.

The beginning of my childhood trauma.

For many years I thought Mum and I were playing a game of hide and seek.

This particular day, I remember I was sitting in the lounge on the floor watching my favourite TV program, 'Play School'. Mum came in calmly and whispered quietly in my ear, "Sharon, do you want to play hide and seek?" I was so excited, I felt my heart racing with excitement. What three-year-old child doesn't like hide and seek, right? In my mind I thought of so many places where we would hide, and I thought Mum would have a great hiding place, as often adults hide in amazing hiding places!

Mum turned off the TV, picked me up and we ran silently to our hiding place. Mum led us to the bathroom. She closed the bathroom door so very carefully and quietly, but it wasn't closed completely and I could see the door slightly open.

Mum stood up looking back at me in the mirror. I stood on the bath so that I could reach looking in the mirror at myself.

"Are you going to count?" I asked Mum.

Mum replied, "Shh, we are playing hide and seek, remember? We need to be quiet so we don't get found."

I then remember looking out the bathroom window and seeing my Daddy's car pull up in our driveway.

"Daddy's here," I said with so much excitement. I could see his orange car in our driveway. I must have heard the car. I watched out the window—obviously he couldn't see me.

Mum continued with the game of hide and seek. She reminded me we were being quiet.

In the next moment there was a thumping on the front door. This lasted for some time. The whole time, I remember my mum seemed so calm. It was like we were really playing hide and seek. She really did a great job at acting calm; not once did I ever feel concerned about anything. She reminded me we were playing hide and seek and made it fun for me.

A few moments later there was silence...

Looking back on this day, I realise at this time my mum would've only been seventeen-years -old! A young woman of seventeen, living on her own with her three-year-old daughter.

I later found out we were in fact hiding from my Daddy, who I'm going to say was drunk. Luckily on that day, he gave up and thought we weren't home. I often wonder how Mum knew he was coming. In those days—now I feel old —they didn't have cell phones to text to say they were coming over, so I guess she just heard his car and had enough time to get me. And then she must have known too that he was going to be angry—how she knew that day that she had to hide is beyond me. I'm so amazed at how my mum at seventeen remained so calm in my eyes and seemed to have it under control that day! She was just a child herself. Not once did she ever look scared or show her actual feelings to me!

I remember many days that went like this—days of yelling, screaming, crying. Sometimes the police would come to our house. Sometimes the front door windows would get smashed. The sound of glass smashing...

I don't have many happy memories in this house. The one happy memory that does stick out for me is when I taught the German boy next door to say banana. He was the same age as me and didn't speak any English. I remember his mum was making him Uncle Tobys porridge for breakfast. We were sitting at his kitchen table. On the table was a fruit bowl with some bananas in it. I pointed to the bananas and said "Ba–na–na." I remember saying this a few times. And then he copied me! I was so excited, I ran home to tell Mum.

I don't have many memories of my dad James. The only memories I have are negative ones. Yet I know I must have loved him and known him to be my daddy because I remember the excitement of seeing his car up our driveway that day we hid from him.

Another strong memory I have of the violence and arguing of my parents was a time when we didn't get to hide. He was at the front door. I could hear the yelling and the sound of fear in my mother's voice. I walked past the door to see if she was okay. He picked me up. I loved my dad. I remember hearing him say to Mum, "I will take Sharon and you will never see her again."

I heard these words and thought, "No way am I going with him." I screamed and kicked him with all the energy I possibly could give. I felt so frightened. I didn't want to go anywhere with him, and I especially did not want to never see my mum again. I looked to my mum to help me. She was screaming. I was so relieved when he put me down, I then ran straight to my room. I can't remember how this day ended, but I can only assumed the police would have come over.

As I grew up I held on to this memory. I always thought I must have hurt him, which is why he put me down that day. I felt so proud. And today, thirty-seven years later, I still don't know why he put me down that day. I'm pretty sure I didn't hurt him, although I am sure I kicked him in the stomach. I just don't think he was hurt by it. Thinking about it now as an adult, what would he have wanted with a three-year-old? I am guessing he was just trying to hurt my mum as she had probably hurt him.

When I was old enough to understand, Mum told me there was a time that he had actually taken me. He drove off with me, the police had gotten involved and eventually he took me home. This I do find scary. I know my daddy would never have done anything to me to hurt me. I know he loved me. But why would he take me, and what did we do while he had taken me? Maybe I'll never know. Even if I asked him, maybe he'll never tell me as possibly he was drunk and will never remember it himself.

Those who know me, know I don't dwell on my past—we all have pasts, right? I am thankful for my past, even though I know it wasn't ideal. For years (I allowed) my past hurt me, and I still do sometimes feel sad for some of the things I missed out on. As previously mentioned, the past, I believe, has helped shape who I am today. Through working on myself and healing, I have accepted my past for what it is, I cannot change what has happened in my past. It is what it is, what it was. It's only with what I do from here on in that I can change.

I never liked violence. I mean, in all honesty, who does? I remember the feeling of shutting down, feeling numb, like I couldn't move. Like the feeling of dreaming—you're screaming, but no sound comes out. Your parents are supposed to protect you, not act like this in front of you.

I know my parents and those around me did the best they could with the knowledge that they had. My mum gave birth to me when she was only fourteen years old, and my dad—who I am going to refer to as James now—was only seventeen. Both of my parents grew up with unforgivable traumatic experiences, with little to no support or encouragement from their parents. James's parents drank a lot, his dad was a fisherman so he was often away at sea. My mum's dad was a workaholic and drank a lot too, and my mum's mum was not a nurturing mother.

When I look back, I think what a past, what an up bringing I had, what trauma. I also think about my parent's upbringing, and how it was history repeating itself.

I experienced an upbringing a child should never have to go through. However, I know I was loved. I know my mum loved me, she wanted to protect me. I also know I was loved by my extended family. And not all the people around me were violent.

Unfortunately, there are other children that go through what I went through—even worse—they're not loved and encouraged like I was. I often think to myself, how do we change this? For me, writing this book, I'm hoping I can get my message out that children matter, and they do not ever deserve to go through any trauma. Trauma effects everyone, especially children.

The cycle can be broken. If you had a traumatic childhood, you don't have to give your children the same life as you. Yes, it is hard. You become what you know. However, you can break the cycle. You can make a conscious decision to give your children a better life. They deserve it. You deserve it.

My Papa, who was my mum's father, did not want Mum to put me up for adoption. He said he wanted to know his first grandchild and promised he would help support her. So, Papa helped raise me and support us.

Helen is mum's mother. All of my childhood memories were of her and my mum always arguing. Helen was unwell, and I think possibly she had undiagnosed post-natal depression or even bipolar disorder. She was not the nurturing mother. She had four children of her own. As her granddaughter, I don't remember having a relationship with her. She never called me by my name—she always called me Karen! I never understood why she did this as I always corrected her and told her my name was Sharon, yet still she would call me Karen.

Mum tells me that I screamed when Helen would hold me, and I would stop when someone else would hold me.

My mum also told me Helen tied her eldest son up and made him eat his food from a bowl like an animal! There were so many odd, strange things that my grandmother did. At some point in her life she did go into a mental hospital, and she may have been diagnosed with something. But it's never been spoken about, so I'm unsure if we will ever know. I just cannot comprehend the fact that my mum's parents condoned her having a baby at the age of fourteen.

Not long after Mum got pregnant with me, she and her family moved to Australia, so I was born in Australia. My mum was just fourteen years old, giving birth to a baby in a country where she didn't know anyone.

Her parents separated, with her mum going to a refuge. My mum didn't want to go to the refuge, so she went to live with my Papa (her dad).

Mum told me she had to take herself to the hospital when she went into labour with me. She took the tram by herself. She was fourteen years old, not really knowing what was happening. How on earth was this okay?

She gave birth to me all on her own. I'm curious as to how this was even possible and acceptable. A fourteen-year-old in a hospital on her own having a baby. Mum told me the nurses did phone her mum, however, her mother told them she didn't know how to get to the hospital. So my mum gave birth to her baby on her own at the age of fourteen years old.

As I sit here and reflect on this, I know it was 1981 when my mum had me—was life really like that forty years ago?

Today if a fourteen-year-old turned up to a hospital on her own to have a baby, I'm pretty sure Oranga Tamariki would be phoned. Oranga Tamariki is a Ministry for children, responsible for the well-being of children in New Zealand.

The story gets better, or worse.

My mum was given gas for the pain—not sure who agreed that she could have it. The nurse gave her the gas and walked out of the room, not telling her how much to have or not have, and she overdosed.

The nurses went back in to see her and shook her, waking her up and telling her it was time for her to push. It's absolutely disgusting that anything like this would happen—it's just so crazy!

Mum told me that she phoned her dad to tell him she was at the hospital and just had the baby. He said that was lovely, he had to go to work, and he would see her when she got home. She really didn't have any support.

When I was a year and half old, we moved back to NZ. James must have heard news that we were back because he tracked us down and stalked us for the first four years of my life.

I can't remember my parents being together as a couple, but I do remember all of the arguing and the fear in Mums voice when he was around. Most of the time she tried really hard to hide it from me, and she was great at it.

From the earliest age that I can remember, when I was three years old, I remember we moved often. I was told this was so James wouldn't find us and torment my mum.

Moving all the time really had an effect on me. I felt unsettled and unsure of what was going to happen in my life next. There are so many pieces to the puzzle I am still so unsure about, I may never know what really happened, or how it happened. There are always different sides to a story. I have only ever heard my mum's side of the story.

When I was four years old my mum met another partner. She got pregnant and had my baby sister. I don't remember much about my sister's father, but I do remember they weren't together for very long, they may have broken up before my sister was born, or not long after. I don't think he really cared too much about us, and I certainly don't remember him caring about me or spending any time with me. And I mean, in all honesty, why would he really? I wasn't his biological child, and from what I can remember I don't think he wanted children. I don't think he was even at the birth of my sister. So my sister also didn't have a dad.

At this point in my life, when my sister was born, I don't remember seeing or having James in our lives anymore. I know we still continued to move often, but I don't recall any more contact with the person I called daddy. And to be honest, I didn't think much about him. It wasn't till a few years went by that he was even mentioned.

Is This What It Feels Like to Live in a Family?

♥

"*Memories made with our family are so precious.*"

When I was five and a half years old my mum introduced me to a man named Sam. He was a nice man, and he was funny.

Sam began to spend a lot of time with us, and we soon moved in with him. We lived in a block of flats, and the flats had a swimming pool. It actually felt like we were in a motel!

Mum and Sam hadn't been together long when one day I asked him if I could call him Dad. I thought, this man is here to stay for a while, and I really like him. My sister was only about nine months old, she only knew Sam as her dad. So growing up she was led to believe Dad actually was her real dad. Her real dad never had anything to do with her. He walked out and that was that.

I remember thinking it was only Mum and I for five years, and then just the three of us when my sister came along. When Dad came into our lives, I remember the feeling of being a family. We went out and did family things together, we had great family Christmas' at his parents house—my grandparents—and my cousins.

Moving houses and relocating to different suburbs was something of the norm. I am not sure how long we would stay living in a house for, but it never seemed to be long before we'd move. I can't even remember the number of houses I lived in, but at a guess I think I lived in at least twenty houses before I was thirteen years old! If you average that, that's not even a house a year! No wonder I didn't feel secure and stable.

By the time I was seven years old, I had already been to two different schools, and then we moved out of Auckland to a small country town called Taumaranui. Taumaranui was about four or five hours away from Auckland by car.

I remember the long drive in the truck. At this age I didn't really understand what was happening, and I didn't feel the effects of changing schools. It wasn't until I was older that I would realise what moving all the time would do to me.

My dad got a job at a furniture shop in Taumaranui, he had friends there, and possibly my parents saw this as an opportunity to start a new life.

So we left our family behind and set off to a strange city. Well, actually I wouldn't call it a city. If you've never been to Taumaranui, there is nothing really there. When we lived there, there wasn't even a McDonalds.

Moving was bittersweet. I was happy that I could have a new bedroom and change my room around, but sad because every time we moved I had to leave my friends behind. Sometimes I keep in contact with my friends, but not always.

I remember Mum being grumpy and yelling at me about packing up my room. I would have to help newspaper the glasses and ornaments, and for a couple of weeks we would live out of boxes until we moved. And then the unpacking of the boxes. Well, this was just as stressful as the packing. Mum always seemed so stressed during both, and I remember just wanting to hide away in my bedroom, pretending I was still unpacking. When she found out my room was unpacked, I had to help out in the kitchen or lounge.

When we moved to Taumaranui, I wasn't too upset about the move and changing schools again. The school I was leaving behind, I hadn't been there for too long—not even a year. I don't even remember if I had any friends at that school. I may have only gone to that school for a few months.

However, the first house we moved to in Taumaranui felt haunted. We would be sitting in front of the fire, and I always felt as though someone had walked in behind me. I would turn around and no one would be there. My sister would wake up screaming in her cot, every night around midnight, for no reason at all. We didn't live in this house for too long—maybe a month. I am not even sure if I went to school at this stage. I can't remember.

We moved out to the countryside, where I caught the bus to school each day. The school I went to was a very small school with only two classrooms.

We might have lived in this house for about six months. Still, I don't remember making friends at this school or being there long enough to make any connections with anyone.

And then—yep, you guessed it—my parents didn't like Taumaranui, so we moved again. Back to Auckland.

This meant ANOTHER change in schools. I don't remember being in the next house for too long or that school either. Possibly not even a year. I'm not even sure if I had time to make friends. I struggled with moving as it would take me a while to make friends, and then just as I started connecting with others we were moving again, and I had to leave them.

By this stage, I began to keep to myself. This was my way of coping. I didn't want to make good friends with anyone. What would the point be?

I would start to make friends and it would be time to move again. So I soon learned to keep to myself and not to open up too much to anyone.

Fitting in was something I have always struggled with, and I never really knew why this was. But looking back, I realise they already had friendships and groups formed at every school I went to. So when a newbie came, it was hard to fit in.

After a few more moves and schools, my parents got married. And then when I was eight years old came the birth of my little brother. My parents bought their first home, and we moved into what I thought would be our forever home.

Life felt really great at this house. I enjoyed my school. I loved this house. I made some close friends and spent lots of my time at the park or mall with them. We were a family. For once in my life, I remember thinking and feeling like I had a family and that life was so good. I felt a sense of belonging, connection, happiness. I can't explain this feeling, it is so hard.

Until I was eight years old I didn't know what it felt like to be a part of a family with a mum and a dad, so when we were a family in this house in Glenfield, Auckland, it was really special, and I really felt loved. I felt like I belonged. These were really some of the happiest times of my life. I remember we would sit at the table altogether as a family to eat dinner! I remember Christmas day feeling special, with Dad handing out the presents. I don't remember my mum and dad arguing in this house, or drinking too much. I do believe when we lived in this house these were the best years of my life. I felt normal, not dysfunctional. And I had my mum and my dad, and to me my mum and dad were happy.

I remember spending a lot of time next door at the neighbours'. They had a young boy. Well, actually he was a year older than me! We were great friends, we used to hide from my little sister! He didn't have the greatest upbringing either. I remember he ran away from home for about a week.

I was so worried about him, my dad was so kind and took me up to Big Fresh, where I thought he would have ran away to as there was free food there! He eventually came home, and life went back to the way it was.

As I grew a little older—I would have been nine years old—I started to wonder more about my biological father. What was he like, what did he look like, did I look like him? I also remember I would put on my sunglasses and imagine that I was talking to and meeting James. I would role-play our conversations. I imagined I would have siblings and a nice step mum. Looking back now, this was my way of coping and understanding my life. Children often role-play to make sense of the world around them, and was this my way of making sense of everything. I don't remember having many conversations with my mum or dad about my bio father. I didn't want to upset them with my questions. I didn't want to be the cause of my family arguing, I loved the feeling of this family!

As much as I know my dad loved me and treated me as his own, I always knew deep down I was not his biological daughter. I was deprived of knowing my biological father, and I don't know how I feel about this. I know it's not my mum's fault, and I don't want to blame my bio father. Why did he not grow up and be a father to me? I remember day dreaming all the time, I would imagine my life to be like my friends lives.

Dad was a great dad to me. I remember him telling me that he would just tell people I was his daughter. Neither of us needed to say stepdaughter or stepfather. It was special that he thought of this for me, but I always knew every time he would tell people I was his daughter, I actually was not. I always felt as if I didn't belong. This was no one's fault, and I don't know how I knew or came to feel this. I knew to "pretend" my dad was my sister's real dad as she had only known him as her dad. And the same dad was my brother's biological dad. But I was old enough and knew, The same dad was not my dad, and we were not related, except through marriage. I remember always thinking I was the outcast, and I didn't belong in my family.

At around the age of eight, my parents became quite good friends with a man, let's call him David. From what I remember, he was a friend of one of my aunts. Anyway, he would come over to our house often, and I remember him teaching me to speak German. I remember he would wear shorts that were so short, and imagining and remembering now, I'm not even sure if he had undies on! During our "German" lessons, I'd be sitting on the ground and he'd be on the couch. Whenever I had to look up at him, which was often, I would see his hairy balls! I never said anything to anyone. I mean, I was only eight or nine years old, and who was I to know what was right or wrong? I was always taught to respect your elders, but in my own thoughts I wasn't sure this was right. But being so young, I had to trust my parents and their judgment in friends.

As time went by, I remember he spent a bit of time with us. One particular day, David and his girlfriend took my sister and I to the swimming pool. He really seemed nice, and we trusted him. I think once or twice my sister and I went back to his house. It seemed like he actually cared about us, but I don't know, I always had this odd feeling about him.

While I was having fun on the trampoline with one of my friends, David turned up at our house in his ute. He came outside to me at the trampoline and asked if I wanted to go with him and my sister to his house, but I didn't want to go. So my sister went with him on her own. At the time she was three years old. I can't remember if it was the same day or a day or so later, but when my sister got home, she asked if we could play Mums and Dads as we often did. She told me to be the nurse and to fix her vagina as it was sore. When she said this, I got concerned. I went straight to Mum. I knew this was not normal behaviour from my sister. Mum sat me down and told me what happened. My sister had a biscuit at David's house, and he had told her that crumbs had gone down her pants, and that he needed to go down and fetch them! So my mum phoned the police and laid charges against him.

This explains why my sister wanted me to be a nurse and fix her vagina. I was so angry with David.

Then my anger turned inward. I felt angry at myself. I remember blaming myself for this for so many years. If I'd gone with them on that day, this wouldn't have happened.

I vaguely remember the day. My sister had to go to court with my parents, but she didn't have to go into the courtroom. But I remember going with mum into the courtroom myself.

A few months later—maybe even a year—I remember Mum sitting me down, telling me not to be jealous. My sister was going to get a pay out of a significant amount of money, and she would be set up for life. I was never jealous, I was just angry with myself. I should've been there. I should've protected my little sister, and I did not do this. I don't think any amount of money would take away the emotional abuse that my sister and our family went through, and I certainly don't think the money has helped my sister in any way.

For years, this affected me. I always felt responsible. I should have been there for my little sister that day, and I let her down. I remember when my sister would sleep, sometimes I would just sit and watch her and feel sad for her. I don't know why, I just felt so sad. I was so angry that someone could do this to such a little innocent child! How could an adult that we trusted take advantage of my little sister?

From memory, he got away with it too, which makes it even more disgusting—he could have done this to other girls. I believe in karma, and I know what goes around will come back around to him.

I'm guessing this situation put a strain on my parents' relationship as it was about then that I remember them beginning to argue frequently. This is where the drinking began. I know my mum was really upset and angry at the fact that this guy had gotten away with it! She was really affected by it. And if it were my child, I would have been too.

On the Move... Again!

♥

"**Trust the future. Trust your family are doing the best they know.**"

My parents began to drink a lot.

I remember my dad would be out working all the time, and I think my mum worked a lot too. Often my little sister and I would walk home from school, but mum wouldn't be home and sometimes we had no way of getting inside. I would suggest that we sit on the back doorstep and wait. I took ownership of my sister; I became a mother to her at such a young age.

Mum and Dad were almost always fighting, yelling and arguing all the time. Looking back now, I don't think they were ever very happy. I didn't like the yelling and fighting. I felt embarrassed. I don't know why I felt embarrassed. Why did they fight all the time? I would just want to run and hide, spend all my time in my bedroom, close the door and pretend I couldn't hear them.

As an adult now, I tend to avoid confrontation. And I still find myself running away to avoid an argument.

And yup, you guessed it! Mum broke the news to me... We were moving! AGAIN! This time I was in my last year at primary school, and we were moving to a different suburb. This meant I would be changing schools again. I didn't want to go.

Having to make friends and fit in was always hard, and when I did finally make friends, it was time to move again. I had made some really great friends. I was constantly out on my bike doing something with my friends. It just wasn't fair! Moving also meant I would miss out on going on camp with all my friends and graduating with them from primary. I was at Marlborough Primary School for three years. This was the longest time I had spent at any school. It just wasn't fair.

This did have an effect on me later in life. I did not have a choice. As an adult now, I find I struggle with new environments for example when I start a new job it takes me months to feel relaxed and build relationships with my colleagues. I don't get too close to anyone I work with, in case I have to leave or they leave.

I knew we weren't moving because of my biological father, as Mum had told me he was in jail at that time. From what I can remember and understand, my parents couldn't afford their house anymore and they had to sell it.

Well, when we moved to the new house, I hated it. It was a state house, as that's all my parents could afford. It was old and cold, and definitely not like the house we had just moved from. I would never want to bring my friends back to this house, I remember thinking. I was so embarrassed. My life had really begun to be turned upside down, and this was just the beginning.

My parents must have been under a lot of financial pressure at this stage, as this is the house I remember the fighting, drinking and arguing got worse. It was really awful. There was so much violence happening in front of innocent children. Infront of their own children.

My dad would often come home drunk. Mum and him would argue and he would get violent. They would yell and scream at each other, mainly it was my mum that was screaming. I would take my screaming brother and sister into my room. I would shut my bedroom door, trying to protect them, cuddling and reassuring them. I can still hear these poor wee kids crying and being so scared. I remember thinking as I would hold my sibling tight—this is not okay, my siblings should not have had to go through any of this. And why did I have to look after my siblings because my parents were too busy arguing to wonder or care what we were doing? This happened often, and I know my mum would wind Dad up (as sometimes us women are great at doing).

Sometimes they would begin arguing, and I would be on the phone with my friends. This wouldn't stop them. They would get louder and louder. I was so embarrassed that sometimes I would end the phone call, or I would close my bedroom door and hide while I talked on the phone. I thought, really, do my parents not care about what other people might be thinking or going through while listening to them arguing? And I think I came to the realisation that my parents were so focused on arguing, they were in fight mode of the brain, using their emotional brain. Not thinking logically. It was like anything could've happened while they were arguing, and they would not notice.

I wanted to be a grownup, be an adult so I didn't have to live in this house anymore. Be a grownup so I could be away from the yelling and fighting. I would often imagine myself grown up and living in a nice, caring home. I remember not wanting to have children when I grew up. If this is what your children went through, why would you have them? I didn't want to give my children the same life that I had.

I know both my parents played a part in the fighting. The arguments they had almost always involved them both drinking. One night, Dad came home from the pub. I was sleeping in their bed. They began to argue as soon as he got home for whatever reason.

Mum came and hopped into bed with me, and he followed. Obviously he hadn't realised I was in their bed. He pulled his fist up to me—but it was supposed to be my mum. She had hid behind me in fear! The anger in his face and the look of fear in my mum's face is something I will never forget.

I don't blame either of my parents. I love them dearly. They were just not good for each other, and they knew how to wind each other up.

I especially remember my dad would warn my mum to stop, but she would keep going, continuing to yell at him. She would get in his way on purpose, like she wanted him to hurt her. She would often accuse him of all these things (and maybe he did them, maybe he didn't). He would be trying to defend himself, but she would manipulate him into agreeing that he did whatever she accused him of. And this often made it worse, as she would say things like, "I told you, I knew it."

Another day, during an argument they had, we were driving in the car, coming back from somewhere. Mum opened the car door during a fight—while Dad was driving! She hopped out. Dad left her there to make her own way home. And it would have been a good hour or two hour walk home. She of course was not happy about this. As a child I was worried for my mum and didn't understand why my dad would leave her. But now as an adult I understand, sometimes you just have enough and you just don't know what to do.

Now that I'm older, I can see my mum and dad both had their own stuff they needed to deal with. When I think of these memories, I have to remember my parents were only in their mid-twentys. The brain is not fully developed in males until at least thirty years old and about twenty–five years old for females! And not to mention, they had three children to care and provide for. They didn't have support from either of their parents. My dad's parents were both alcoholics. I don't remember them ever coming to visit us. We always went to their house.

I don't know much about my dad's up bringing, all I really know is he was second to youngest and had 8 siblings. And his parents also liked to drink a lot of alcohol.

In the new house, I remember walking home from school one day. On this particular day when I got home, Mum said she had to talk to me. She explained to me that James, my biological father, had attempted to jump off the Auckland Harbour bridge. He was on the news! I watched and did not really have any feeling to this. Probably the only feeling I had was feeling so embarrassed and hoping none of my friends would ever find out that he was my dad! I never spoke about this to anyone; I don't even remember showing much of an interest with my mum. I didn't know what to say or think, apart from feeling embarrassed,

The story was that he had stolen his sister's car and taken his girlfriend to a beach and raped her, dragging her by the hair along the beach. Then he drove her to the harbour bridge where he stopped the car in the middle of the bridge, hopped out of the car and threatened to jump off the bridge. I watched as a police officer talked him out of jumping. He was hanging over the side of the bridge! The police officer managed to talk some sense into him, and he didn't jump. He did however end up back in jail, I think he got about seven years in jail.

Throughout most of my childhood, I remember my parents going out and often they would forget their house key and not be able to get in the house when they came home, so they would knock on my window for them to let me in. I would scream and get really frightened as I would think it was James coming to kidnap me. I remember this happened on at least two occasions, with my parents whispering "Sharon" both times as they did not want to wake up the whole household. Thinking about it now, I don't know why they didn't wake up the babysitter, but maybe they knew I was a light sleeper. I knew my mother had the fear that James would take me one day. But this really did have a traumatic effect on my life. In fact, this affected me all through my adulthood as well. Any little noise I would hear, I often thought it might have been James. I would wake up and look straight to the window, looking for a person, that person.

Often when I would walk places, when I would be walking by myself, especially when I was the ages of nine and ten years old, if I saw any men walking towards me on the same side of the street I was on, I would cross the road in panic that they may have been James or possibly they knew James and would take me to him. I'm not sure if something must have happened at this age for this feeling to be instilled in me, as I don't remember feeling like this before living in this house. At the house we lived in previously, I was always at the park (as we had a park behind us) and always by myself and never had trust issues of men there.

Growing up from when I was nine years old, I lived with this fear all the time. You see, I never knew what James looked like, so I was afraid of every man since any of them could have been him. It was only when he went to jail that I remember feeling safe. Whenever he was out of jail, Mum would seem scared that he would take me.

Mum probably should not have shared her fear with me. I know she was protecting me. I'm sure she didn't realise the effects it had on me, but she needed to make sure I was safe. Today at the age of forty – one, I still have this fear. This is something I am working on and hoping to overcome. Later in my story, I will explain how I faced my fear, inspired by the saying, "If you have a fear of something, then face it."

So it's important to remember that if you do have fearful thoughts, don't put them onto your children. I know my mum didn't know any better, and she didn't realise the effect it would have on me. Children, no matter what age are affected by everything that happens to them. It may not affect them at the time, but the effects will show later in life and can show in so many ways—addiction, depression, history repeating itself.

It wasn't until I was eleven that I became more curious about James, and I got to meet the man who at the age of three I had remembered to be my father. I met him in jail. I remember beginning to be curious—and don't get me wrong, I loved and still love my dad—but I was always curious and wondered, did I look like this man? What was he like? And why did he try to kidnap me at the age of three but put me down when I kicked him?

Mum had been asking me if I wanted to meet him. And to begin with, I didn't. She told me it was okay if I wanted to. I thought it would be a good idea, so she arranged for me to have the day off school and to go to the prison to meet him.

I remember walking into the prison and feeling like royalty while I got special treatment. It really didn't feel like a bad experience meeting my 'daddy' for the first time. It had been organised that I met James in an interview room with one of the wardens. I was glad as this way we had a bit of privacy, and I didn't need to be surrounded by the other prisoners. Although I didn't see the other prisoners—I felt scared of seeing them.

James was not what I expected him to be, but then I didn't remember what I expected him to be. It was a strange feeling. I think I felt numb—I didn't know how to feel or how I felt. He looked like a nice human being.

I remember asking him why had he put me down the day I kicked him when he tried to take me from my mum, and he said he couldn't remember. The only questions I had to ask him and he said he didn't know the answers and he couldn't remember! I always wondered if it was just that he didn't want to have that conversation with me or did he actually not remember?

He said I was so beautiful, but I didn't care about that. I don't remember what I even felt. This guy is my biological dad, but he has never actually been a dad to me. He felt like a stranger to me. He was a stranger.

It would be a few years before I would go back and see him again, and this was only because my aunties (his sisters) and Nana wanted me to go and see him with them every Sunday. I really wanted to have a relationship with my family, my cousins and aunties. And I thought that if I wanted a relationship with them, well, then I had to go see James on Sundays with them. They never told me this was the case. This was something I had thought of in my own mind. I think I only went twice, and I didn't enjoy it. Walking into the prison with all the guards watching you, then the prisoners. They all looked so scary and threatening. I always felt uncomfortable and unsafe.

I really wanted to be a part of what I thought was a normal family, so I went with them. After visiting him and having this horrible sick feeling in my tummy while I was there, I decided I never wanted to go back there again. So I stopped contact with my family. I thought that I had to do that, as I was too scared to tell them I didn't like going to that place. It wasn't them or him, it was prison—not a very nice place for any child. I never told my mum why I wanted to stop contact, I just told her I wasn't ever going back there again. Mum was good and didn't question or interrogate me, she knew I didn't like to talk about things. I bottled things up inside.

Not a Family Anymore

♥

"The sign of true forgiveness is when you stop wishing it had been any other way."

Not long after I met my biological father in prison, after many years of my parents fighting and being very abusive towards each other, my mum ended her marriage with my dad.

One day after school, Mum told me we were going to stay at her friend's house as her and Dad were separating. I remember telling my friends my parents had gone on holiday and I was staying at a friend's. I was so embarrassed that my parents were separating. What would my friends think about me? All my friends' parents were together, and they had such happy families. I was also so angry at Mum. Why was she willing to break our family up? Even if it was abusive, it was the only thing close to a family that I had.

It wasn't long after that I became angry at my dad. I was so confused! I just wanted my family to be together. I longed for a normal, loving family. I had a picture in my mind how I thought a family should be, and that's what I wanted. Kind of like it was in the movies. But I had to accept this was never going to be the case. Even though deep down I knew my mum and dad were no good to each other together, I didn't want to live with the shame that they had separated and having to explain that to others.

A week or so went by, and we then moved AGAIN. Luckily, this time we were in the same area so I could continue going to my school! Dad would pick us up to take us out on Sundays. I never wanted to go because I was so angry with him. I don't even know why. I think possibly Mum had been saying things about him. But then Dad would say things about Mum, and I would get so confused, trying to put all the puzzle pieces together. It really was so hard not being able to work it all out and piece it all together. Even today, I still do not know or have all the answers, and maybe I never will.

A few months went by, and all of a sudden, my parents were getting back together. Well, at least Dad was staying over a lot and there was lots of drinking going on, and they spent lots of time in Mum's bedroom. I remember going in there sometimes, and yuck, the smell! I can still smell it today—the smell of stale alcohol. I began to get frustrated with this as my mum would begin to leave us kids to fend for ourselves a lot more. She really began to have no time for us. Well, not like the time she had when she was on her own. I must admit, I began to act out. I didn't like the way my parents were, they were not giving me or my siblings enough attention, so I began to misbehave in order to get their attention.

I remember I would sit in my mum's car that was parked up the drive way. Sometimes I would pretend I was the mum, and I would be dropping the children off at school. I would tell them to have a nice day and to have fun. I would chat away. Sometimes Mum would come out and ask who I was talking to. "No one, Mum," I would say. And I would feel so embarrassed that she had heard me talking to myself.

My parents getting back together didn't last too long. They began arguing and fighting again. And before I knew it—yup, you guessed it—we were moving again.

A Big Move to Palmerston North!

"Trust the future."

This time we were moving to Palmerston North, which is a small city seven hours away from where we lived in Auckland.

My dad tells me he turned up one Sunday to pick us up, and the whole house had been cleaned out. It was empty. All our furniture was gone. He said he was devastated. To this day, I do not know how true this actually is, and to be honest, it doesn't matter. I have no remorse or blame towards either of my parents, as I have said, I am just sharing my story of how I lived and saw my life.

Mum had met a guy down there and moved us all to a little village called Rongotea. I had about five weeks left of Intermediate school. I wanted to stay in Auckland to finish my last few weeks, but Mum said I couldn't. So this was another school I did not get to graduate from.

I went to Rongotea School, which was a small country school. Trying to fit into a small country school was really hard. The principal was horrible—on my first day, he really humiliated me and said something along the lines of, "Surely, a young girl from a big city will be very smart." And then he asked me to answer a really hard question. I had no idea what the answer was! I was so embarrassed and felt so small. I was not smart at all, I struggled at school. I had no clue where I was up to with my schooling because I was forever changing schools, and each school teaches different things differently and at different stages. And with all the fighting and abuse going on in my household, it's no wonder I struggled to retain any information or learn anything. My mind was always focused on what was going to happen when I got home.

I think by the time I finished my schooling, I counted I had been to eleven schools over my childhood. I vowed and made a promise to myself that I would never change my children's schools! And to this day, I have stuck with that promise. So, a piece of advice if you do have to move and change your children's school, prepare your children, involve them as much as you can in the process. Think if you are going to move, how many more times will it be likely that you will move. I am not saying you shouldn't change your children's school, just make sure you aren't going to move them constantly. Obviously, life happens and some things can't be helped. I am sure if your children are involved in the process and you discuss the changes with them, they will be fine. I had other dysfunctions in my life, not just the moving!

We didn't live in Rongotea for long, Mum didn't like being stuck out in the country. Mum's boyfriend, let's call him Doug, was HORRIBLE! He was a control freak. I get it that he had structure and wanted things his way. My poor little brother was very scared of him, and I don't blame him. Doug was scary at times. My little brother wet his pants one day in fear of Doug. He would have only been three or four years old. It was terrible.

I grew to stick up for myself, and I remembering telling him often I didn't care. At this stage, I was a teenager and felt like I was a victim. I hated him. He would threaten to send me to boarding school. I asked if he could, as boarding school would surely be better than living with him. He never sent me.

Throughout these years, I don't remember talking to my dad too much, and I certainly don't remember him visiting us in Palmerston North. I think Dad continued to have a relationship with my brother (who was his son) but he stopped talking with my sister and I. I do remember talking to him on the phone once. Doug was sweeping the kitchen, and he swept rudely over my feet as if I was in the way. He didn't like my dad, and he certainly didn't like that I had a good relationship with him. Maybe that was why Doug was so horrible to us. But to this day, I still don't really know why my sister and I were not included with our dad and brother. It was almost like we didn't exist anymore.

For my thirteenth birthday, I remember my dad saying he would try his best to come down for my party. I was so excited! However, on the day, he did not come! Mum said she had a surprise for me, and I was so excited thinking it was Dad. But when I got home, it was a small group of my friends in the living room. I was very surprised—and also very let down! It was the one thing I so badly wanted. I don't remember talking much to my dad after this. In fact, I think mainly it was only my brother who would talk to him.

I cannot remember how long Mum and Doug were together, but it felt like a lifetime. I know I was a grumpy teenager, and this showed in so many photos of me. But I really did not like Doug. I honestly could not see what my mum saw in him, and I could not understand why she wouldn't leave him, knowing her children did not like him.

And then, it happened... Doug and Mum separated—yippee and finally! However, this meant we were moving, again.

After Mum and Doug separated, Mum began drinking again almost all the time and I was left at home to look after my brother and sister. She would go out often, and sometimes she would not come home till all hours of the morning. In the mornings before school, often I would make my sister and brother's lunches and get them ready for school before I had to walk myself to school. You see, at this age, my mum would have had three children aged thirteen, eight and five, and she would have only been twenty-seven herself! Some people at the age of twenty–seven haven't even had their first child yet—let alone having three children and one being thirteen years old! And I wasn't the most well behaved thirteen-year-old at times. At school I would act out to the teachers. I had little trust in anyone, especially adults.

I remember a few times when I ran away from home. One time I left at some odd hour of the morning, like 2:00am! I stole my little sisters' bike (which had a puncture) and rode it to my boy friends house (mum was trying to stop me from seeing him), still wearing my pajamas too might I add, so classy. What on earth was I thinking? How did I think I was ever going to get away with it is beyond me. Of course, my mum found me that morning and I was in a hug amount of trouble.

So, I understand that my mother was trying to live her life. She was struggling, and she did the best she could with what she knew. Maybe I was a trigger for her at this age, as I was the age she would have been when she got pregnant with me, it didn't help that I was doing rebellious things and acting out. Things were good some times, mum was fun when I had my friends over. I do remember more times that were not so good. Mum met and started dating our neighbour, he was a really nice guy. His nephew and I were in the same class at high school, and we were mates. But this relationship also had it's dark stories. They drank a lot, and other stuff too, which I was so embarrassed by!

On this particular night I was babysitting my brother and sister, and mum wasn't home (as usual). I cannot remember what I was doing in

Mum's room, but I found a letter written by my mum that she was going to end her life and what she wanted for us children. I was so worried and phoned for help. A lady came over and spoke with us and my mum. I was so worried Mum was going to get so angry at me for phoning for help. But I didn't know what to do. She didn't get angry at me. And she didn't end her life.

Phoning for help was hard for me to do, I was just thirteen years old. But at the time, I didn't know what else to do. I couldn't talk to Mum about the letter, so I phoned for help. If you are ever put in this situation, always seek professional advice.

Then not long after this, I lost my virginity and told my mum. She lost it with me, and she punched a hole in the wall. I had never seen my mum so angry and so violent before. I was so scared. Who was this woman? I had seen my mum and dad fight and yell at each other, but I had never seen my mum so angry like this before.

A few days later, after school one day, she took me for a drive and broke the news to me that she needed a break. She did ask me if I was okay with going away for a couple of weeks. My siblings and I wouldn't be going with her. We would be going to a family home in Bulls, which is a half an hour's drive from where we lived.

At the time, I was very supportive of this and I knew that Mum was struggling. I didn't want to miss school, as I was at high school. I had moved so many schools, I could not bear the thought of leaving another school. I had started to make some really great friends. So I went and stayed with one of my friends. It was, after all, only going to be for a couple of weeks. However, after the two weeks, Mum needed more time. So, two weeks then turned into three months. Then after three months, it turned into forever.

At the age of thirteen, my siblings and I were separated and put into foster care. I always remember thinking at the time this was my fault—if I hadn't found the letter, if I hadn't... It was a lot to carry for a teenager, who should have been out enjoying life with her friends. And not to mention learning at school! I never did well at school, I could never concentrate. As I have said before I always thought of my home life.

Bruce Perry, author of *What Happened to You?* is a trauma expert who says that "dysregulated children will not learn." Frustration, anger, fear can shut down the cortex part of the brain. It makes sense to me now why I did not learn at school. I was always in stress mode and constantly feeling unsafe.

After a couple of months, the holiday stage was over. I began to miss my mum and siblings. I remember one day after school, I decided I would just walk to Mum's house instead of getting on the bus to go home. I missed my mum so much and thought it would be fine to just go and visit her. Well, this was not the case. I was told Mum wanted a break from seeing us, and I wasn't to turn up at her house. This hurt so much. How can a child not be able to see their mum when they needed them? I was a teenage girl, trying to feel a sense of belonging, a sense of connection. And the connection I did have was with my mum. Even if it wasn't a positive environment, it was the environment I was familiar with.

After a few weeks of Mum having the break she needed, I was able to go back to visiting her and at times staying a night or two with her. From memory, I think I began to stay on the weekends, and my siblings would come and stay too. Because I was a teenager, I didn't really put the time and effort into spending quality time with my brother and sister. This is something I regret and think about often. I also remember feeling resentment towards the close relationship my brother and sister had with each other. They were almost joined at the hip and did everything together. They had each other. I felt like I had no one.

After about three months of living at my friend's house, my friend and I began to fight. We were in the same classes at school and shared a bedroom, so it was no wonder we started to argue. Soon, I had to move to another foster home.

The new foster house was so awful! The foster mum smoked A LOT at the kitchen bench. Infact thinking now, I am not sure I saw her anywhere else but at the kitchen bench smoking. I saw and experienced a lot of things at this house I should not have. It makes me sad thinking about it, that children are placed in foster care in hope of safer environments, and this is not always the case.

One night (on a school night) one of the daughters and I went around the corner to visit one of her friends (I think they were about twenty years old). They pressured me into spotting up - with a cap of oil. I didn't want to, however they would not stop, so eventually I said okay. They gave me a spot, but it didn't do anything so they gave me another. That also didn't do anything, so after a few more... I was experiencing the worst experience I have ever had! I honestly thought I was going to die. I told them I needed to go to the hospital as I had a hole in my head. One of the guys told me just to think happy thoughts. He told me I was okay and to look up to the stars. It honestly was such a horrible scary moment. Let's just say, I have been put off drugs for life! That night we got home about midnight, and I slept on the couch.

The foster mum never questioned me or said anything! In the morning I got up for school, on the walk to school, I still felt like I had a hole in my head and that everyone was looking at me funny. How is something like this even allowed to happen to a child in foster care??

Things didn't improve here. I can't remember how long I lived here for, maybe a year—it certainly felt like forever! I babysat for one of their friends. Her partner had just got out of jail, and he was at the house while I was babysitting. He got quite scary and asked me if I had ever had sex, and he began to corner me. The phone rang—I think this saved me.

I ran to get the phone. I never babysat for them again. I told my mum what had happened, and she came and got me. Mum got into trouble from the social worker for taking me when she wasn't allowed to. But no one was listening to me. I had told the social worker how bad it was at this house, but I still had to stay there. I never felt listened to. They didn't listen to me.

It was at this foster house that I attempted to end my life. After having an argument on the phone with my mother, and a boy I was dating at the time also broke up with me. I felt rejected and worthless. My mum during our argument had told me I wasn't welcome at her house. I decided I would take a whole heap of pills. I remember taking them and then beginning to feel bloated so I left the last one, but (I can't remember how many I took, maybe twenty-something. I went for a walk with one of the boys who also lived at the foster home to get some fish and chips. Sitting there, I began to feel so ill. I started feeling dizzy and felt drugged. I told him I had to go home. I went home and told the lady what I had done. She had to take me up to the hospital, and I had to have my stomach pumped. It really was a horrible experience! The nurses shoved a very thick tube down my throat, placing black charcoal inside my stomach. This would make me vomit – and boy did I vomit! All over the hospital floor. Was this what my life was going to be?

A lady came and spoke to me, asking me questions about why I'd taken all the pills. She seemed really nasty and not very nice at all. She questioned why had I left one pill, like she was insinuating that I didn't really want to end my life. I remember at the time thinking, lady you have no idea what my home life is like, you have no idea what I live with every day. No, I didn't really want to end my life, I wanted help, I wanted someone to listen to me so I didn't have to live in that foster home anymore.

I remember the foster mother saying to the nurse that her children do not stay in hospital and I would not be staying. The nurse said I had to stay as I needed to be on IV fluids. I stayed and was in hospital for three days. The whole time I was in hospital, my mum did not come and see me, and she didn't phone me either to see if I was okay. I remember asking the foster mum if she had heard from her, but she hadn't. And when I did finally hear from her, she was angry with me. And it was all about how could I have done that—on the same day her partner was in a train accident and his friend passed away as a result. I remember at the time feeling so angry as she was always played the victim. And could she not see I was crying out for help? I didn't want to live at that house. It was so terrible, yet no one was listening to me!

But eventually, I did get to leave that house—eventually they started listening to me. Although I had nowhere to go, I told them I had to go. They put an advert in the newspaper looking for somewhere for me to live, and in the meantime, I went to a lovely lady for about two weeks. Then from the advert, they found a lovely home for me.

Between the ages of thirteen and fifteen, I lived in four different foster homes—but it felt like I had been in foster care for so much longer than that! Every day felt like a month.

The last foster home I lived in was really nice. They were a beautiful family. However, it was not my family and I didn't feel like I belonged. They were so loving, always out doing things together. I always imagined and had wanted to be in a family just like this one. I was not used to a loving family like this, it felt so strange for me. I remember thinking to myself, what the heck is this? Do they really seriously all love each other this much and are always so nice to each other? This was not normal. Not normal to me. I was not familiar with living in a home like this. I really struggled, as it was not my family. I felt really bad, as I know they genuinelly cared about me, and they wanted me to feel a part of the family. But no matter how loving and kind they were, they were not my dysfunctional family that I was used to.

It's a strange feeling living in someone else's family home. There's not really any sense of belonging. There's not the connection that you have with your family. Don't get me wrong, I was grateful for this family. What I wanted and needed was *my* family. The need for a sense of belonging. Even though the house I was living in was stable and loving, I didn't feel like I belonged, I didn't fit. It was traumatising for me.

Adding good relationships to your life doesn't fix or erase the broken relationship or the trauma. The experiences and trauma of your past will always be there, you cannot just erase or get rid of the past. You can however create new positive experiences. And talking to a professional will help you change your mindset and build new healthier pathways for the future.

It takes time to heal from trauma, sometimes many years. Years of creating new positive experiences and relationships. Offer understanding and be patient with anyone who is or has gone through traumatic experiences. They will be feeling that the world is chaotic so when they are surrounded with calm, they will likely act up, creating the chaos. Subconsciously they will be looking for evidence that people cannot be trusted, that they don't belong.

I decided that I would move back in with my mum, who had mentioned a few times that she wanted me to move home. By this stage, my brother had moved to Auckland to live with his Dad. I barely saw my brother or sister.

There was a family meeting. My sister's biological dad was phoned and involved in the meeting. So Mum had to break the news to my sister that Dad was not her real dad. I am not sure how this went. I have never really spoken to my sister about this.

My sister had continued living in the same foster home, although she had moved up to her dad's at some stage for a while. It didn't work out up there with her bio dad. They are Jehovah's Witnesses and lived a completely different life to what my sister was used to, so she moved back to the foster home that she had always been at. I remember feeling resentful for my brother and sister as they were younger and had more stability then I did. They both had families that they had been with the whole time. They kept in really close contact and saw each other often.

My brother told me when he was older that he didn't know I existed when he was young. I guess for me, I always remembered and saw a lot more. I don't know if this was a good thing or not. My sister always seemed closer to her foster sisters then she was to me, and of course she would be. She lived with them longer than me. But this hurt me so much. I always just wanted to be a part of a loving family, I wanted my family to be a family. I felt like my brother was lucky because he had his dad and step mum. And my sister had the same foster home she went to at the very start. This family became her parents. She was only eight years old when she went to live with them. She called her foster parents Mum and Dad and her foster sisters her sisters. I remember feeling so hurt and betrayed; I was her sister. I should have had a close relationship with her, not her foster family. All I longed for was a family, my own family.

At the end of fifth form (third year at high school) at just fifteen years old, I decided to leave school. I didn't spend much time at school anyway. I never sat any of my exams at the end of the year, so I left with no qualifications. No one really knew how much I was struggling as I kept my thoughts and feelings to myself. I didn't feel listened to anyway. The only thing I remember liking about school was being with my friends and giving the teachers a hard time. Oh and visiting the school councellor, Mr Riely almost daily.

Mum has always said I could leave school, but I needed to get a fulltime job or do a course. I opted to do an Introduction to Early Childhood Education course.

Living with Mum I think only lasted about six months. My mum was always out drinking and partying, and sometimes I would come home to knives that had been on the stove where she was spotting up, with oil in caps. I was so against this after my own experience, I threatened to call the police. And I was so embarrassed that my mum would do stuff like that! We were constantly arguing about this.

Sixteen Years Old—and PREGNANT!

♥

"*A* ccept yourself for who you are."

Before I decided to move out from Mum's, I met Andrew. While I was out 'boy racing' during the weekends with my friend, we meet some nice boys from Foxton. I can't actually remember how, but we hopped in their cars and went driving with them all around the square. Looking back now, I think this is so crazy and irresponsible!

My mum would go out almost every Friday night. We would wait for her to leave the house, and then we would walk to town. My mum would have no idea that we were out! And we knew she wouldn't be home till at least one in the morning, so it gave us plenty of time in town, driving around with boys we didn't know!

Mum and I had an argument one day, which was not unusual. But this particular day, I had decided this was it. I packed up my things and told her I was moving out.

I moved in with a friend and his mum. I still continued with my course. But then this all changed. Life changed.

I can't remember exactly how long we were together before I got pregnant. At sixteen, I found out I was pregnant! I was taking contraception, and I was being careful and responsible. However, for whatever reason, the contraception did not work.

I remember going to a lovely doctor, thinking, what am I going to do? I didn't want to have the same life as my mum had, but I couldn't bear the thought of having an abortion. I was not old enough to really think of what having a baby actually meant. I would have to give up my course. But at the time, I did not think of the effects of this.

When I told Andrew, he was supportive and said we could do this. He was four years older me, so maybe he could! He said he would support my decision. I was sixteen years old, thinking I was an adult, thinking I had my life in control! Wow, did I have a lot to learn! At sixteen, I did not look at the bigger picture. I didn't look too far into the future. I never imagined that I would one day be old and would not be with Andrew, and that this baby I was having I would have to look after for at least nineteen years! I never once really thought about the consequences of having a baby at just sixteen! Looking back now, I think oh my god! What was I thinking? sixteen years old, that's just a baby!

Having to tell my mum I was pregnant was one of the scariest things I have ever had to do. I felt so sick and scared. I knew she was not going to be happy about it—and in all honesty of course she wouldn't, she was just thirty years old herself! Of course, she didn't take the news well at all and didn't speak to me for some time. I knew she needed time to process and that she was probably disappointed, not only in me but in herself. History was repeating itself, and I know she didn't want me to follow in the same footsteps that she had.

Eventually, maybe a couple of months later, she did come around and she tried to be supportive.

Andrew and I decided to move in together. However it wasn't long before I started to notice his anger issues. One night, he put a fist up to my face. I told him not to dare ever hit me, because that would be the one and only time I would let him. He never did that again.

The night I went into labour, Andrew, my foster mum and sister had been at a New Year's Eve party. We got dropped off at home around 1:00am.

We walked in the door. Andrew and my foster sister went to bed. I had this strange feeling—I went to the toilet, and it just felt strange. I phoned my foster mum to tell her. She asked if I had been bleeding or had a show. I didn't know, so I went back to the toilet, and yes, I had a show. I don't remember being scared, I think I just had no idea how much my life was about to change! I really was a sixteen-year– old acting like I was twenty-five.

This was also one of the times Mum and I were not talking to each other, which happened often. Just like her mum and her mother.

My friend's mum said she would come back in to get us and take us to the hospital. She asked if I was going to phone my mum, but I said no. She talked me into phoning her. She said I may regret it if I didn't. So, I did. And Mum met us at the hospital.

At the hospital, not a lot was happening. My waters had broken, but I was not having contractions. It would be at least fifteen hours before I felt any form of contractions.

Andrew fell asleep on the floor. My foster sister and Mum went home to have a sleep. They came back in time to be there for the birth.

As it got closer, Mum suggested I have some pain relief. I didn't want pain relief. I was so against any form of drugs. I did not like the feeling of not being in control.

However, as things progressed, I was getting tired. My doctor explained that pethidine would be fine to have and would just help me sleep during contractions. Mum was worried I would be too tired when it came time to delivering the baby.

So, I agreed and had the pethidine. Then, it was all on. This was it. After fifteen hours, I gave birth to Sally. My baby. She was absolutely beautiful.

She was just perfect, weighing 7 lb 7 oz. I loved her from the moment I saw her. She was, however, sleepy from the pethidine. And to be honest, so was I. She slept all night.

I stayed in hospital for a couple of days. One of the nurses commented how I was doing such a great job. She mentioned that I knew to change the baby's nappy, that I didn't ring the bell to get the nurses to change her nappy. She went on to say that there were older mums in their thirty's who did this.

Taking our baby home was scary but also exciting.

Mum came over with my brother and sister. She bathed Sally for me. I was a little scared to bathe her; I was worried she might slip into the water.

All my nights were consumed by Sally—broken sleeps, feeding, winding, changing and rocking her back to sleep. I didn't know how to get her to sleep, so I used to rock her in my arms. Later on, we used to have to take her for drives in the car to get her to sleep! I soon learnt this was not a good idea!

I remember that my little sister, who would have been eleven years old when I had Sally, wanted to take her for walks. But I was so protective. I wanted to prove I was a good mum and that just because I was sixteen didn't mean I couldn't be a good mum.

I gave everything to my baby daughter. I was a good mum... Well, at least I think I was most of the time. Being a mum was hard, getting up through the night, not really knowing what I was doing, but knowing I had to nurture this baby and attend to all of her needs.

In the very early days, I signed up to a course called PAFT (parents as first teachers). A consultant would come over once a month and go through where Sally was at, what milestones she should be at. She gave me advice and support on activities to do with her and was there for any other advice I may need.

I found this really helpful. And it was nice having someone to talk to, because all my friends were still at school. They didn't have children so I found that I was becoming isolated from them. The high school I went to was just down the end of the road I lived on, so in the early days of having Sally, a few of my friends would call in on their lunch break. But mostly I lost touch with them, as they were off doing teenage stuff—stuff that I should have been doing—while I had to focus on being a mum.

When Sally was about eight months old, I did go to a young mums play group, which I found helpful. But I struggled to connect with the mums. They already had their groups, and I think joining their group like this was a trigger for when I had to start at a new school. This reminded me of the friendships that were already formed at the schools I went to. Most of the mums' children were three or four year olds, so I could not relate to the conversations they were having, such as toilet training. I hadn't experienced any of that yet!

I had no idea how having a baby at sixteen was going to affect me. Being sixteen years old and having a baby, I thought I knew what I was doing. I didn't realise how much my life was going to change.

Fear From My Mother

♥

"**A**ct from the heart."

One morning, very early might I add, around 6:00am... I woke up to the phone ringing. Who the heck is phoning at this hour of the morning? On the other end of the phone was my mum. She was beside herself, and I couldn't understand a word she was saying. "Mum," I said in a motherly voice, "Calm down, I can't understand you."

"He's here, Sharon, he's here. I can smell the alcohol on his breath," Mum replied at a hundred miles an hour. She was almost hyperventilating. I could hardly make sense of what she was saying, but I knew she was in fear!

Okay, so I worked out the person she was talking about was my bio dad, James. After I managed to calm my mum down, she explained... She had woken up to a voice message on her phone. He had phoned during the night, and luckily, she had slept through and not answered it. He was phoning to say that he thought he might come over for a coffee!

Then she started working herself up again and not making any sense. I managed to calm her down again and told her not to panic. I told her chances are he would have called her, probably drunk, from Auckland, planning to drive down and not have made it... She calmed down. Once I was happy that she was feeling okay, we hung up.

When I got off the phone, I decided that I would go to the police station just to get some advice and see if someone would go around and talk with my mum to reassure her. I dropped Sally off at day-care. I didn't want to expose her to any of this trauma, she didn't need that.

When I walked into the police station, I asked the policeman who was standing at the counter if I could talk with a woman police officer. I was weary of men, probably due to my fear of James.

I sat and waited in the waiting room, thinking about what I was going to say.

A lovely policewoman opened the door, walking towards me and smiled at me. "Sharon," she said. I nodded so nervously. She led me out the back of the station, down a short hallway, into a private room. She pulled a chair out for me to sit in. She shut the door behind her. She sat down. She had hold of a pen and notepad, ready to begin writing. I didn't know what I was going to say. I didn't know how to start this conversation. I had only just turned eighteen, I remember. I felt all alone. I was just a child, all alone, talking to someone I didn't know, with no support. But I was brave. I had to do this. I had to for my mum.

I took a deep breath and told the policewoman I was here about my father. I gave his full name. To this day, I still don't know why I did give his full name at first, but it's funny how things turn out. The policewoman looked at me and gave me this look like she knew who I was talking about... In my mind, I thought, "What? Does she know James? How could she, he lives in Auckland."

So I asked her if she knew my father. I was really confused, wondering how she could know him. She told me, "Yes, he's here. Are you here to bail him out?"

Oh my god... What... What did she just say?! How is this even possible? How is he here?

I explained to her I was not there to bail him out and told her what had happened. My mind was going crazy. What would I tell my mum? I had told her not to worry, that he would not have made it all the way here... How would I tell her? I couldn't phone her up to tell her, she would need someone with her, she wouldn't be able to drive...

The policewoman told me he was just a block away from my mum's house, on the same street she lived on!

The police had pulled him over as he was driving erratically. She said he was a very angry man; he was above the drinking and driving limit. They arrested him. It took about six police officers to hold him down and get him in the police car!

What had I just heard? Was this actually happening? I felt like I was in a movie. I had to pinch myself a couple of times to remind myself this was real!

How was I going to explain this to Mum? I couldn't phone her and tell her on the phone that he was here and to come to the police station. I was worried about how Mum would take this news. She wouldn't be able to drive to the police station.

I explained to the policewoman my dilemma and that I was worried about Mum going into shock and not being able to drive to the police station if I told her why she needed to come to the station.

I called Mum and told her to come to the police station, that I had come here for some advice. I would wait till she got here to tell her that James was here... locked up in the police cell!

When she arrived, I had to assure Mum that the policewoman was lovely and that we could trust her. I told her what had happened, that James was here, locked up. Mum took the news as I expected, the fear in her I can still remember today.

One thing we all said was, "Wow, someone was looking after her that night!"

He was picked up by the police just a block away from my mum's house! What would have happened if the police had not picked him up? I could not bear to imagine the thought.

Did James drink while he was driving all the way from Auckland? The drive from Auckland to Palmerston North is a good six or seven hours' drive, and only if you don't stop! All that mattered now was that he had not made it to Mum's house and she was safe.

It might have been the next day, I spoke with the police woman and I asked if she thought it would be a good idea if I went and saw him and told him to stay away from us. She told me that was very mature and brave of me.

So the police woman and I made a time for this to happen. I remember going into the cell to see him, and I couldn't even look at him, I told him I had all I needed in life and to leave us alone. I did not make eye contact. I did not want to make eye contact with him. I thought if I did this, he might not believe how serious I was being.

He asked how my baby was.

"I have come here to say what I need to. I don't need to say anymore," I said very confidently and sternly. I started to walk towards the door to leave. However, the police officer told me to wait there while they took him out. And that was that!

I honestly felt like I was in a movie, it all felt so surreal. Again, reflecting on this, remembering this day, I had never thought of it, but the fact was my mum was only thirty-two years of age and she lived by herself. This would have been so extremely scary for her. I will never forget the fear in her voice that day when she phoned me. And I had only just turned eighteen! My youngest daughter is almost seventeen years old now. I could not think of her or any of my daughters being in a situation like this on their own without their parents or an adult to support them.

The Breakdown

♥

"Remember you are worthy, competent, loveable and very special."**

About two months later, when Sally was about sixteen months old, I thought being in a relationship with Andrew was not what I wanted. However, it took me many times to break up with him. I was eighteen, living with this guy that I no longer wanted to be with. I had never broken up with anyone before and did not know how or what to say!

This particular day, I remember it being Mother's Day. Andrew had brought me some flowers, which he rarely did, and put them next to me in bed. I had been talking to friends a couple of days prior, and I had mentioned this time I was going to tell him. I felt so bad when he had gone to the effort to buy me flowers. But I knew if I didn't do it, nothing would change. And I was unhappy. I decided not to discuss this with him on Mother's Day.

The next night, not long after Andrew got home from work, we sat in the lounge watching TV and I thought to myself, Sharon, it has to be now. You can do this, you have to do this. I took a big, long, deep breath. I could hear and feel my heartbeat racing so fast!

I was sitting on the couch; he was sitting on the chair to the right of me. I turned and looked at him. He was watching TV. I asked him if he would hate me if I told him I didn't want to be with him anymore. He looked at me. There was a long silence, the look of disappointment, hurt and anger on his face. He did not take this too well. Who ever does when they are on the receiving end of a breakup? He didn't really say anything.

In fact, he didn't talk to me for about three days, and then he left to live with his mum. However, he would still call in every day on his way to work—he worked just around the corner. I thought he was coming to see Sally.

Once he turned up in the middle of the night with his sleeping bag, saying he couldn't sleep. He asked if he could stay the night. I didn't want to give him false hope, so I told him he couldn't stay. This was extremely hard for me, but I knew I had to be strong. I didn't want him thinking we were going to get back together.

My mum and I have always had a love-hate relationship, and I have often been the mother of her. If you have ever watched the TV programme that used to be on years ago, Absolutely Fabulous—which is a British program where "Patsy", the mother, is desperate to stay young and her daughter "Saffron" is constantly taking care of her mother, being the responsible one—a lot of people would refer to me as the daughter and to Mum as the mum on that programme. And it is so true! I am the sensible one, with my mum being... Well, more adventurous! I know my mum did her best with the life that she had and the best she knew how.

Often we would have an argument and go months and months without talking to each other. We would have some outrageous fights, yelling at each other. Looking back, I don't really remember what we used to argue about. I think we just clashed, and both have completely different opinions, values and beliefs.

I didn't really feel as though I had support from her, and I couldn't really tell her what was going on. I knew too that Mum didn't like Andrew. He was clingy, and I couldn't go anywhere without him. I know this annoyed Mum. I felt all alone... I mean none of my friends had babies, they were still at school, and I didn't know how to relate to them anymore. I also tended to bottle things up and not share too much of how I was feeling with my friends.

At the age of eighteen, I had a breakdown. I was living on my own, and I began to isolate myself from my friends. I was getting myself into financial debt, as I had brought a car that I should never have brought, but I thought I knew it all! I was not eating, and looking back at photos, I looked terrible, so skinny and sick! I was feeling all alone, and I didn't know where to turn. I didn't know who I was or who I wanted to be. I had lost all direction. I had hit the bottom, and at eighteen years old, did not know how to find my way back to the top.

I felt so confused and numb. What was going on with me? Am I going crazy? Why do I feel like this? To this day, I still don't really know what caused the breakdown, I guess it was a mix of all the things going on in my life. The childhood upbringing I had and the lack of stability and family was obviously affecting me. I gave up my job at KFC, and I left my Early Childhood course. I didn't want to leave the house. What was happening to me, I thought. I felt so alone. Yet I also know I had created the loneliness. I had pushed everyone away.

At this point, Mum thought the best solution would be to give my daughter to Andrew, just for a short time. Andrew agreed to take her. He suggested we go into the courthouse and let them know that I was going to hand over full custody to him. I remember we walked in, asked the lady behind the counter for the forms and began filling them out. "Shall I write that you will give our daughter back to me when I am better?" I asked him.

But he said no, "We don't want them to think we are playing games with her." And I fell for that! I trusted what he was saying.

After we filled out the forms and handed them to the lady, she mentioned that we would be assigned a counsellor. I do not remember ever being assigned a counsellor. And to this day, I think it is absurd that they let this happen! For one thing, I was in no state to be signing a legal document, and two, how did they know that the father wasn't holding a gun to me, telling me I had to do this? I was eighteen, with no knowledge of how the system worked or what I was doing. I was not in any frame of mind to be making any legal decisions! And little did I know that I would have to fight for years and years to get my daughter back!

This is a great example of how history can repeat itself. My mum suffered from depression and struggled with her three children. She gave us up for foster care. Little did I know that five years later, I would be doing the same with my daughter.

In most situations where child trauma has been present, the chance that their parents or their grandparents had gone through similar trauma is highly likely. According to **Bruce Perry**, who is an expert on child trauma, trauma are patterns that run through a person's life and often run through their parents' and grandparents' lives too.

I most certainly did not intend for this to happen, as I'm sure my mum didn't either. I know the effects being placed in foster care had on me and the trauma I endured. But here I was now, being in similar shoes and feeling similar to how my mum would have been feeling when she made that decision to put us in foster care. I most certainly empathise with mum and know now she would not have made her decision lightly. History repeating itself—the good news is though when recognised, the cycle can be broken.

Often, we are quick to judge decisions or actions other people take, not knowing when we may be faced with the same or similar situations. Until we are faced with a situation ourselves, we cannot really say what we would never do if we were in the same situation. Until we go through an experience, we cannot completely empathise with that experience.

None of my friends knew what was going on or what I was going through. I was so embarrassed that I'd had a breakdown, that I had given my daughter to her father. That I had failed as a mum. Who does this to their child? What would everyone think of me? For years and years, I really struggled with this thought. I had to live with what happened every day of my life. I was still able to keep in contact with my daughter, and eventually, I ended up taking her to kindy (kindergarten) every day and brought her back to my place after so we could spend more time together.

Distraction, Maybe?

♥

"You are amazing. Believe in yourself."

It wasn't long after I hit rock bottom that I met Richard. Well, I already knew him as he was in the same group as Andrew. We had been great mates since I was fifteen years old. One day I thought, I like this guy more than as a friend. He lived out of town but worked in town.

One day I suggested to him to stay at mine, he did, and well, I needn't say anymore... We too had a bit of a rocky start to our relationship as he would get close to me and then break up with me, crying, saying it was him not me!

How did I attract these guys! He enjoyed different things to me. But I didn't really care, I liked him!

A year after we started dating, I got pregnant. But we weren't really together, we always had a strange relationship. I always thought I was not good enough for Richard, as he always looked at other girls and made it obvious if he wanted to 'hook up' with them, even when I was pregnant! I had little self-esteem and thought this was all I was worth, so no matter how many times Richard cheated on me, I still stayed with him, hoping one day he would love me just like I loved him. Richard and I broke up for a while and then got back together. This happened often. With Richard randomly telling me if we were out, "We are not together Sharon". At first I thought, this was news to me. Then I quickly worked out he had spotted a girl he had liked and wanted to dance with her.

Anyone who is feeling negative thoughts about themselves or has low self-esteem, or even allows others to put them down, please know you don't have to do any of this. You can overcome these feelings, as I did. With determination and positive thinking, you can feel better about yourself.

Richard got into two separate relationships (at separate times) with other girls while I was pregnant. He continued to live with me, but also stayed with them a few times or as much as he could.

His first girlfriend, I really struggled with and I became a person I did not like. I ended up receiving a trespass notice from the house she lived at. I was not proud of the person I was, but I was hurting, and I just couldn't accept what was happening.

Just before we had our daughter, Richard said to me he was willing to give us a go and he wanted to be in his daughter's life. At the time, I thought, I have been given a second chance to be a good mum, I know I am a good mum.

Things were great after we had our daughter. At least for a while... Then it wouldn't be long till he would cheat on me again. And I would forgive him. As mentioned earlier, I had very low self-esteem and thought that's all I was worth. All I had longed for was a family and to belong. And I thought this was my chance.

I go back to the feeling I had in the loving foster home, how I wasn't familiar with this environment, the feeling of love. And with Richard, I felt this was normal and what I was used to, the emotional abuse was what I was familiar with.

I was not always a saint. Often when Richard was planning to go out with friends on a Saturday night, when he would go take a shower. I would get in the car and take off, leaving our daughter at home with him. This was in the hope that it would stop him from going out. If he didn't go out, he couldn't cheat on me and not come home.

I used to interrogate him like you would never believe. All of the time, especially when he would get home from a night out.

Richard was not always supportive, especially when it came to my family. One particular time, I remember we were in town shopping when mum's friend phoned me, to tell me mum had taken some sleeping pills. She had to leave to go to work, but she had phoned an ambulance that was on its way. I remember thinking, how can I tell Richard what has happened? And when I did, he responded how I thought he would.

I remember walking into my mum's bedroom, seeing her pale, looking half dead on her bed. I remember the feeling of anguish come over me. I didn't know what to do. My bones felt like they were crumbling. I wanted to fall to the ground. I paused, my body couldn't move. I couldn't believe what was happening. Richard left me as he was going out to town, so I was all alone. The ambulance came, and I went with them to the hospital. Mum was barely responding, it really scared me.

At the hospital, I had to take on the mother role again, but I was used to doing this. I remember thinking, why? You weren't there for me when I had done similar. Why should I be there now? I felt so angry.

The nurses and doctor pumped her with charcoal. She woke up. I guess she would have been disappointed with herself. Still to this day, I do not know what happened, why her life had got to the point where she wanted to end it. And maybe I will never know. Maybe it doesn't matter.

Do we ever know why life gets so bad that we want to end it? All I know now is when something like this happens, you go through many emotions and you think and wonder what was going on inside their brain to leave so many people hurt with unanswered questions.

There are options for you if you are feeling so bad that you want to end your life. Please phone someone or call the suicide phone number in your area for help. There are options other than ending your life. How you are feeling right now in this situation is not how you will always feel. Talking to someone about how you are feeling, or even if you don't know how you are feeling, is so important.

One Saturday night while we were driving around with one of Richards friends, we stopped at my friend's house. At the time, Emma and I didn't really know each other that well, we had just met at young mums group. Well, Richard told me they were going into the party, and I was to stay in the car, that I was not to go in! And being the person I was back then, I listened and did as I was told. Often I felt a sense of judgment when I would talk, as he would often talk down to me. I can see him looking at me, know the look he would give me.

After six and a half years, just after my twenty-fourth birthday, after many times of Richard and I breaking up and getting back together, I finally decided we were both so different, we both wanted different things in life. And when our daughter was three years old, I told him this was it, I couldn't be with him anymore. This was the hardest thing for me to do, as I loved him so much. I asked Richard to move out.

Somewhere deep down inside of me, I knew I was not achieving what I wanted to or was destined to, while I was with him. Plus my self-esteem was so low, that I did not speak when we went out to parties – or anywhere. Richard led me to believe that I had to sit in the corner, that I didn't belong.

Looking back on our relationship now, many years on, I see we were toxic for each other. We both played mind games and treated each other with no respect. We didn't have any respect for ourselves, so how could we show or treat each other with respect? It took me ages to be strong enough to work out we could not be together, and this was so hard because I had loved the idea of us being a family. I had a vision of what I wanted for our family. And no matter how badly Richard treated me or spoke to me, I loved him and would do anything to keep us together.

After Richard moved out, there were times he would say he missed me and I would miss him, there were nights I would invite him over. But deep down, I knew I should not give in to this. I needed to find myself again, I needed to remember the person I was. And the person I was when I was with him was not the person I wanted to be. Richard and I are still great mates; we have both grown up and apologised for the way we had treated each other.

We both share our beautiful daughter together. And have both provided her with a stable and consistent life.

Richard and I were both too young to settle down, let alone have a child!

Richard has a beautiful partner, together they share a child. We all often share family occasions together. Richard and his family are a part of our extended family, and we are a part of his. This on it's own has been great for our daughter. Even if at times, she has told me how weird it is that we get celebrate some occasions together!

Feelings of self-worth, or lack of, can be affected negatively by trauma as well. You can overcome these feelings of lack of self-worth. I will explain to you how and give you some exercises that may help when you are in these situations. It's never easy to change our thought patterns, especially when they are thoughts about ourselves, so be kind to yourself, allow yourself time, and work hard every day on changing your negative thoughts to positive thoughts.

Value yourself.

Many of us are guilty of comparing ourselves to others, and with social media, we always see how amazing everyone else's lives are! How beautiful they look! And when we post a photo of ourselves, we look at it and think doubtfully, "Hmm..." We are our own worst critics. And we SHOULD NOT be! There will never be anyone else in the world just like YOU.

Recently, I heard about a lady who was on a zoom call every day for I think it was a week with the same people. Every day she wore the same top to see if anyone would comment. But not one person noticed or commented! It's so true, isn't it? That we notice all the negative things about ourselves? Maybe we think, our hair doesn't sit right or something looks bad... But, guess what? Everyone is so worried about how they look that actually they don't really notice how we look (or that maybe our hair is out of place). We are all too worried about ourselves! How often do you judge or think negatively about your friend? I know I always think about the amazing people I have in my life and how great they look. But we still do it, still compare ourselves to others when we shouldn't.

So again, we are often too critical of ourselves, we are our own worst critics.

Try telling yourself one nice thing about yourself every day for a week, and then the following week, change to something else nice about yourself. See what happens.

Who are you? Who do you want to be known by? Write down who you are, all you qualities. Write down these qualities as if you already are . For example, "I am kind and caring and have a great shaped bottom." Value yourself.

It sounds really crazy, but... Look at yourself in the mirror, saying, "I am good enough, I am amazing, I am confident, I am..." Say this to yourself every day. Positive affirmations do work when you say them out loud to yourself every day. You'll start to believe; notice and watch your views of yourself change.

When you notice or think a negative thought about yourself, very quickly replace it with a positive thought. Yes, I know what some of you are thinking: this is easier said than done. But when you start to say positive things about yourself, you start to feel positive about who you are.

I too still have unwanted thoughts enter my mind every now and then. I stop when I catch myself with these thoughts. I remind myself these thoughts are not my way of thinking anymore and I replace them with a positive thought.

If you promote a healthy, positive self-esteem, you'll be more confident. This will show in the way you are around your friends, your family and even people you don't know.

When you try something there is an element of failure, just do it.

Meeting Stu

♥

"*The start of writing a new script: the princess and the prince*"

At the age of twenty-four years old, not long after Richard and broke up, I met Stu, the person I call my husband today! Stu changed my life. Stu has helped me feel confident, he has always seen the good in me, lifting me up. There is so much more I could say about my relationship with Stu over the past eighteen years, but this book is not about that! Maybe one day I might write about our drama free relationship and what I think makes it work.

In the beginning when I met Stu and began spending time with him, I felt so confident, and don't get me wrong I still do today! I really opened up to him and told him about my relationships, my self-esteem issues, about my childhood, my fears. He was so loving, so supportive, encouraging and always listened. He still is all of these things and more! When I was with Stu, it just felt so right. I felt as though I could be myself and I was not judged. Stu has always said to me to be proud of my past, to be proud of all that I have achieved. He has a great way of helping with my self esteem. And I know he believes in me.

There is something, though, that I do have to tell you... Stu is sixteen years older than me! So, when we spent the night together—the next day, I thought, oh my god, what have I done! He was forty, I was twenty-four.

He was not the type of guy I would ever have gone for. But yet, it felt so right.

Stu treated, and still treats me, like a princess; he is always so thoughtful and knows the right things to say.

Stu was also my boss's brother. Eeek! So in the early days, we didn't want people finding out, as we both didn't want to be in a relationship, so we snuck around and didn't tell anyone we were dating. It was so exciting, sneaking around like children.

Richard had come over to see our daughter at my house one day. He was starting to get suspicious that I was seeing someone. He got hold of my phone to read my messages and saw the messages to and from Stu. He, of course, was hurt and angry that I was seeing someone else. At this time, it was completely over with Richard and I, but in the past, we had broken up and got back together numerous times, so I guess he thought it would be the same this time too.

In some ways, I believe meeting Stu was great because if I hadn't, I might have gone back to Richard again, and who knows how my life would be today.

It wasn't long till we had to decide to either make a go of our relationship or to end what we were doing. Richard's boss was my boss's partner, and once she would find out—well, our whole workplace would find out. We decided to give it a go and we told our coworkers.

One thing that really stands out about what was different with this relationship was we set boundaries right at the beginning. Stu and I both told each other what we did and didn't want. We had both been cheated on and did not want to live like that again. Stu said he didn't like game playing and jealousy. We agreed we both wanted a great happy life. I knew this relationship was different, I knew he was the one.

Don't get me wrong, in the beginning we did come very close to breaking up. Every time we would argue—I was moving out. I thought that every argument we had would mean Stu wouldn't want to be with me anymore. I had grown up watching my mum leave every time her and my dad had argued. I had never been in a relationship or had role models that talked through there issues rather than run away from them.

Then uh-ohhh—I fell pregnant! Stu didn't have any children of his own. And I wasn't sure I could have any more, as one of my kidneys was dysfunctional. When I had my first daughter, it had been picked up that my left kidney only functioned 8%, and during my two pregnancies, I had gone to hospital on many occasions with urinarye infections. When I had Jasmine, my second child, the doctors had mentioned that I may not be able to have any more children as it may have an effect on my health.

Stu and I had a lot of deciding to do! We both agreed to wait to make our decision till after we had spoken to the doctor to see if my kidney would cope.

It seemed like a long wait for the decision on if my body would cope with having another baby or not. I felt so bad for Stu; I knew he had given up on the idea that he would ever have his own child, so this would be his final chance.

Then finally the day arrived that we would find out if we could or couldn't go through with this pregnancy. The doctor said I could have the baby, and I would be monitored closely each month at the hospital.

We were doing this. We decided we were having a baby.

Stu had always acted as a father to everybody else's children, but he had never had his own. He had his ex-girlfriend's daughter living with him. He had taken her on, as her mother unable to care for her at that time.

A few months went by, till we decided I should move in with him. So Jasmine and I moved in. I was monitored closely with the pregnancy. Everything was going well.

Because of my kidney, I was induced two weeks early. So at 38 weeks pregnant, we went to the hospital to be induced.

My midwife put this gel type stuff around my vagina, which I believe is to help start the contractions. Not a lot was happening after they induced me. From my experience with Jasmine, I knew that once they broke my waters, it would be all on. I mentioned this to the midwife, so she broke my waters. And that was it, it was all on.

At one stage during pushing, the midwife told me I needed to stop pushing. The baby had her hand up by her ear. She couldn't come out like that, as this could dislocate her shoulder and cause serious harm to me. Our baby had already taken a breath though, so it was a little complicated.

I stopped pushing, and the nurses put pressure on my stomach trying to turn the baby. And, wow, this was the most worst pain I have ever experienced! Luckily, they achieved what they needed to, and a few minutes later, I gave birth to a beautiful baby girl. She was, however, blue.

They placed her on me, and I fell in love instantly. Then a nurse put an oxygen mask over her face, not saying anything. They gave the mask a couple of pumps and then put it back. But... then... out of nowhere, another nurse just whisked her off me, over to the table. Another nurse put her two fingers on my baby's chest, pumping her heart, with the oxygen mask back over her mouth. What? I thought, What was happening? No one was saying anything. If they were, I couldn't hear what they were saying.

I watched over, thinking, no, this is not happening. I did not just give birth to a baby to lose her. How would I cope with losing my baby?

The nurses didn't seem worried, and they all seemed to be working so well together. How they knew she had stop breathing is beyond me. I guess there was no time to sit and explain to me what was happening.

It felt like forever. I wanted to hold my baby. I wanted to feed my baby. I wanted to hear my baby cry. Why was she not crying?

And then, the wait was over. We heard the cry we'd been waiting for. Our beautiful baby girl cried. The nurse handed her to me. Everything was okay, she was a fighter. I was so thankful for the nurses that day, so grateful that they knew what they were doing. So grateful that I got to take my baby home and so grateful that she was healthy.

After a few months had passed, I went to what I thought was going to be my final appointment at the hospital to get discharged for my kidney. I went there on my own.

I sat down and waited for the sign off. Instead, the doctor said they had a DHB meeting, and it was agreed that they would remove my kidney. Um, what? What did the doctor just say?

The doctor had said that my kidney was only functioning at 8%, it was causing more harm than good being left there. I asked him what did he think had caused this kidney to stop functioning like this. He thought that I would have had recurring urine infections as a child that had gone untreated.

So that was that. He said he would make an appointment for surgery in about eight weeks' time.

I left the appointment. While I was going down the lift, I phoned Stu. I cried and cried. This was not the news I had expected.

The next eight weeks felt like the longest eight weeks of my life. I had so much anxiety. I had never had an operation before. I didn't like the feeling of being drugged. How would this go?

For the next eight weeks, I began losing weight. I was eating normally. I went to the doctor to ask if he could put me on pills to calm my nerves, but he said it was only six weeks and I could do this. I could get through this without pills.

And I did.

The day of the surgery I did not speak. I could not speak. I was so nervous. The anaesthetist could see this and suggested I have a relaxant pill to help before the surgery. This certainly helped.

My doctor has told me that I will live a normal life with just one kidney. And after I recovered, I began to put on weight again and felt healthy. I just have to drink lots of water, and I am not allowed to have anti-inflammatory medication or multi vitamins.

You see, I could tell you all many more life experiences that I went through, but that would require another whole book.

I learnt at a very young age how to be resilient, and that success is built upon effort and determination. I also believe having a vision, knowing what you want in life and what you don't want in life, is so important.

Later in my life, I learnt the importance of relationships, especially positive relationships. One thing I can tell you is I know I have always been determined, and I always knew I wanted a better life than what I had growing up. I didn't want to give my children the same life I'd had.

Once I get a feeling or an idea about something I want in life, I keep going and keep striving until I succeed. Even if at the time, the thing I wanted had not always been the right thing for me, which leads me to the next chapter on resiliency—having the coping skills to make it through those difficult moments.

Self-worth can often come from traumatic experiences that we have been through, just like an abusive childhood or relationship. It's so common to have these thoughts about ourselves, to have these doubts:

"I am not good enough."

"I want to be tall."

"I want to be thin."

"I want to be fun so people will want to hang out with me."

These are many of the thoughts I have had over the years. These thoughts can be overcome! You can change your thinking and feeling. A friend of mine, **Anthony Semann**, once said, "Saying negative things about yourself is a form of bullying. You wouldn't say those things about your best friend, so why do you say them about yourself?"

And I ask myself all the time now, "Why am I so worried about how I look or what I'm thinking?" I am the only one that is worried about it. We're the only ones that worry and think negatively about ourselves, right?

You can change your negative thinking about yourself into positive thoughts. This takes practice and determination every day. Every day you have a negative thought come into your head, wipe your hand across the top of your head and say to yourself cancel. Cancel the thought. Replace the negative thought with a positive thought. This takes lots and lots of practice and time, but it's so worth it!

She's Coming Home

♥

"*What's Meant to be Will Find its Way to You.*"

After meeting Stu, having our baby and then going back to work, I really felt as though life was great. We were having Sally stay with us every second weekend. Although there were times that we had functions on; for example, each Christmas our work would put on a Christmas party for the children, with Santa being there handing out presents. But if this weekend would fall at a time that wasn't our weekend to have Sally, she wouldn't be able to come with us.

I really struggled with this. Jasmine and Sally were really close. They were like best friends. And of course, Jasmine would tell Sally at school she had been to a Christmas party. This was one of the many things Sally missed out on.

Things were not so great at Sally's dad's place. I had taught Sally our phone number and told her to phone whenever she wanted.

One morning she phoned, saying her dad and his wife didn't know she was on the phone; they were still in bed. She had been playing in the mud and was now cleaning her feet in the toilet.

I would phone up to talk to her, with her dad's wife calling out to her, telling her, "Sally, Sharon is on the phone for you." This hurt me, as I am her mother. I felt she purposely would say Sharon not Mum is on the phone. I thought it to be very manipulative. Another example when I thought she was manipulative, she phoned Sally on her birthday – however the whole conversation was about what she had been doing with Sally's brother, not once did she say happy birthday or ask how Sally was.

One night when we had Sally, Stu was bathing the girls. He noticed Sally had a welt on her bottom. He asked her what had happened, but she said she didn't want to talk about it. He told her to show it to me.

She came down and showed me. We sat and talked for a while. She eventually told me she had forgotten to take her lunch box out to be emptied, and her dad's wife had smacked her with the wooden spoon.

I had to be so strong. I could feel the tears welling up in my eyes. I never smacked my children. How could someone who was not her parent smack my daughter?

Nothing really happened with this, there was not a lot we could do about it.

A few weeks went by.

I was dropping Jasmine off to school. It was her first day. We went to find Sally, to get some photos of Jasmine and her together. Sally was hiding her right eye. She was shaking. I of course asked her what had happened. She said, "I don't want to talk about it." But then she told me it was the dog. For some reason, I did not believe this. I went straight to Stu at work. He phoned the Ministry for Children, and they investigated but could not find anything.

Maybe a month or so went by, then one afternoon, just out of the blue, Andrew phoned.

"Sally will be coming home with Jasmine tomorrow," he said

"What?" I replied.

"Sally wants to be with you, so she is moving home tomorrow." Andrew said.

And that was that.

The next day when I picked Jasmine up from school, Sally was with her too. Sally said to me she could not believe she had said that she wanted to come home with us and her dad had agreed. I could see the weight off her shoulders. She was also concerned about her dad and hoped he was okay.

I was absolutely over the moon. I had all three of my girls home. Sally was ten when she came back home to us. Sally mentioned to us on a few occasions that living with us felt like a dream, she said it didn't feel real. I was so proud of her for the courage she showed the day I picked her up from school to come home to us.

The feeling of having all my girls together, a family. We were a family. My daughter Sally did not have to miss out anymore.

I remember times it was hard for Sally, as she had different rules at her dad's house. Even though she didn't live with her sister all of the time they were close.

Sally wouldn't talk to her dad for a few months. She didn't want to see him. We let her have her time to process the situation. Her lawyer had said she couldn't go to his house when his (now ex) wife was there. It wasn't too long till they separated, and Sally began going back to her dad's for visits and weekends.

When Sally was sixteen years old, we had an argument, and she went to live with her aunty. She didn't speak to us for a couple of years. These were the hardest two years of my life.

Sally's aunty is Andrew's sister and wasn't very supportive or encouraging for her to keep the relationship with us.

I would text Sally often and get myself so worked up. I would cry every day, wanting my daughter. Wanting my family.

Sally eventually came back into our life with the help of her dad, who encouraged her to. She was about eighteen years old. I am so grateful for this. Fast forward to now—2022. Sally is twenty-four years old and has two daughters of her own, which makes me a grandmother of two beautiful little girls. And Sally is a fantastic mum.

Resiliency

♥

"You are strong, you have got this—being resilient gets you through the hard times."

Resiliency for me is having to get through, knowing that you have to get up every day—but you would rather hide away. But resiliency is what helps you get through. You know you are tough, strong—you tell yourself, "I have this, but is it always going to be this hard?" Resiliency is the ability to cope with and recover from challenging experiences, or traumatic events. Challenging experiences or trauma affects us all in different ways. What I can cope with compared to what you can cope with may be completely different. For some people, just getting out of bed on a daily basis is being resilient. Building resilience takes time, strength and support from people around you. Never ever judge someone's lack of or strength in resilience.

If you, or anyone you know lacks resiliency, they will likely feel overwhelmed or helpless, relying on unhealthy coping strategies (such as avoidance, isolation and possibly turn to alcohol or drugs). If you are feeling any of these things, the great news is you can train yourself to be more resilient. This takes time, and consistency. Some of the ways you can build resiliency are; surround yourself with a good support group of friends or people that can help you with your challenges, learn different coping skills – including journalling, changing your thought patterns, breathing exercises, and mindfulness training can help with regulating your emotions, thoughts and behaviours.

My papa was my idol; he was my only constant. In my early childhood, we lived with him and I remember spending lots of time with him. He was always fun, he always spoilt me.

Before we moved to Palmerston North, Papa would take my two cousins, my brother, sister and I out every Sunday. This was always very special. We would always get $5.00 pocket money, scratchers and a lotto ticket.

When we moved to Palmerston North, at my leaving party, he didn't know where the house was. He wanted to come and say goodbye to me, so he walked up and down the street yelling out, "Shaz." I heard this and went out to see what was going on. It was so cute. He had come to say goodbye to me.

Papa would visit us in Palmy most years. He wanted to retire here in Palmerston North and had told his work mates that he was going to retire here with his granddaughter.

Being the eldest grandchild, Papa and I shared a special bond. He did tell me he didn't have favourites, but there was something special about your first grandchild.

In 2016, I lost my idol—the most important person to me in the whole wide world, my papa.

In life, nothing ever prepares you for when someone close to you passes away.

Papa was like the father I didn't have growing up, although, he was more than that. He was someone I admired so much and someone who had always loved me unconditionally. I always knew growing up if I ever got married, it would be my papa who I would have walk me down the aisle. And I am so fortunate to have had this happen. I remember on the day being so nervous, I started to cry. Papa said, "What are you crying for, love?"

Like I was silly for crying! I am so grateful that he got to walk me down the aisle—this is definitely something I hold so close to me.

I had a connection to Papa like no one will ever understand, a really close bond. Even as I begin to write about him now, the song "(I've Had) the Time of my Life" from the movie *Dirty Dancing* came on and I burst into tears. I remember watching this movie at his place every time I visited as a young child; it was his partner who first introduced it to me. I said to my husband, I am so silly! I have not cried for Papa for a good while. Why am I crying now?

When someone you love or care about passes away, it's important to be kind to yourself, allow yourself the time to grieve. And if you find that years down the track you still cry at the sound of a song that reminds you of that person, this is completely normal. There is no amount of time that can go by that will make you 'get over' it. You never really 'get over' the death of a loved one, you just learn to adjust and live without them.

Often bringing out photos or thinking of fun times and memories you had of that person is a great tool—let your tears out and go with the feelings that you are feeling. Be kind to yourself. I have not lost my partner or a child, so I have no idea what that feels like! I am sure the grief of a child would be very different! But surround yourself with close family and friends and allow yourself the time to go through all the emotions.

So back to resiliency. When I found out my papa was unwell and might not have too much longer to live, I had just began my journey to starting my own business, the childcare centre. I knew the day my papa was going in to find out his results, and normally I would have phoned him. But I didn't want to know the results—I guess I already knew. My brother phoned me and told me Papa was waiting for me to phone him and that he said he hasn't heard from me for a while.

Driving on my way back to work from lunch, I thought, okay, it can't be that bad... You have to phone him, Sharon. And... Well, let's just say, the news was not good—he had cancer again. But I was still in denial.

If you knew my papa, you'd know he was a fighter. He worked right up until six weeks before he passed away, driving buses in Auckland! We had meetings at the hospital, and I made sure I flew up to be at all the meetings. A lot of family drama happened, as it does when there is a death in the family. But my papa got his one wish, which was a photo of him with all of his children together!

I know I did my papa proud; I was there for him in the hardest of times in his life. I spent the whole day with him at the Auckland hospital when he had his first day of radiation. The doctors suggested someone be with him, as he may not understand or hear very well. I was the best person for this job. And it was the best day I had, getting to spend the whole day with my papa.

I remember the night before, he even told me what time to leave and which way to go! I was driving his car, and he told me to drive it carefully! During his radiation, he slept and got tired. There were calls back and forth, and I was keeping my family updated. At one point, my uncles from Aussie phoned and then my mum. I walked to a different room to avoid disturbing Papa. However, when he woke up a few hours later, he asked me what was I arguing with my mum and uncle about? I thought, are you serious? How did you know that? There is no way possible he had heard as I walked some distance to talk to them! I can only guess that he was soul travelling—I am not even sure if this is a thing! But it was so strange that he knew what was going on!

It was not too long after this that we were all sitting around him, spending our last few moments with him while he took his last breath. I was so fortunate to be there with him on this day, and I am so grateful that the universe allowed this to happen! My poor little sister did not make it, and I can only imagine the pain she feels that she was not there sharing the experience with us. Although, I'm a big believer that those who are passing choose who will be there with them when they pass, and they choose those who they think are the strongest to cope with that situation.

When Papa passed, I was very sad, but I also had no regrets—as often some people do. I had taken lots of videos of our conversations, lots of photos and I had told him everything I wanted to tell him. I know that he knew how much our relationship meant to me. He also told me he could never thank me enough for what I had done for him. I was at peace, and I know he was too.

Most of my life, I have always been the strong one, the one who looked after my brother and sister when my parents fought, mothered my mother, and then at the time that my most important person in my life had passed away, I too had to be strong. I am known as the family organiser, so if anyone wanted anything organised, they would just come to me. And yes, you guessed it—I had to organise my Papa's funeral. (Well, I didn't have to, but I needed to.)

I had already talked to him about what songs he wanted and in which order. We had organised for Papa to come back to his sister's house, and I slept next to him. This process really helped me grieve. My mum lost it when we had to put the lid on his coffin on his funeral day—and as much as this was hard, I had to be strong and lead the way. I had to be strong and tell her it was time to say goodbye, we had to put the lid on the coffin. After his funeral at the crematorium, when they began to lower his coffin into the ground, this is where it was my turn to lose it. For me, this was the end, the final moment. This is where I really thought life was unfair, and I was not strong anymore. I ran out of the room, hyperventilating. A person who worked at the crematorium must have seen this happen before, and he distracted my thoughts. Before I knew it, I went back into the room and held myself together.

I think it was at this moment that I realised all my life I had been resilient, and I had thought one of the reasons I had been resilient was because I always had my papa who believed in me. He had loved me unconditionally. So now, everything I did I was doing to make Papa proud, although what I learnt was that I was resilient and that I was working on everything for myself. I could get through this—I had been through many tough times in my life and still managed to remain strong and not easily damaged. I had got back up and continued on.

At times, I was not sure how I managed—however, some tools that may help you could be talking with your family or friends with how you are feeling; allowing them to be there for you; and ensuring you take time out for yourself.

When a relative is unwell and in hospital, it can be tiring and draining. We focus all our energy on being with this person that we forget to be there for ourselves. It's important to take the time to look after ourselves. Feel the emotions, cry when you need to cry. Let it out. Enjoy all the moments you have left with the unwell relative. One piece of advice I was given was to record conversations I had with Papa. I did this, and I still watch and listen to those videos.

Today, whenever I feel as though I am not strong enough, I think of my papa, who when he was really unwell, said to me, "I am not ready to go, it's going to take a lot to kill weeds." My papa was a fighter, he worked hard right up until a few weeks before he died. He taught me resiliency, how to fight, to have principles stick to them and what I believe!

There are many stories throughout my life that I could talk about where I was resilient. I believe I must have been resilient from such a young age, as from as young as I can remember, I had managed to recover or adjust to many changes that occurred throughout my life. I think also having emotional attachments with my mum, papa and then my dad when I met him at when I was five years old, helped with building resilience. I will talk more in the next chapter about what research says about what resilience is.

But for me, I don't really know for sure what has made me resilient. I can only guess as a young child having my mum and papa always there for me, encouraging me and helping me succeed helped build the foundation for when I was in foster care and fending for myself. And then the determination that I had for a life I had always dreamt about—I remained focused and kept hold of that dream. My husband always reminds me of this, and I hope this can help in some way for you as it has for me.

If you are going through hard times, remember that there was a time in your life that you weren't going through hard times, and remember that how you are feeling throughout this hard time is not how you will always feel! In one, three, or even twelve months from now, you will be in a totally different place—more positive and happy—and this hard time will be just a memory of the past.

What defines resiliency

Research I have looked at has talked about resilience as being the capacity to recover from difficult events, to fall down in life but make the decision to keep moving forward. Its like climbing a mountain without knowing how you're going to get to the top. Getting to the top takes time, strength and help from those around you. Once you do reach the top, the view is amazing and you will look back at how far you have come and will be stronger than you were before you fell. I know this has been the case for me; when I have been struggling to get to the top of the mountain.

I remember a friend of mine referring to some of our struggles with the song, "The Climb" by Miley Cyrus. And at times, I would turn to this song's words: "Gotta keep tyring, gotta keep my head held high..." I highly recommend to anyone going through struggles to listen to this song or find a song that inspires you too! This song helped me when I found I was struggling. I would turn up the sound and sing along as loud as I could, really getting into the song. I still today listen to this song whenever I am struggling.

It is believed that having a healthy attachment relationship during childhood, emotional regulation skills, and being able to visualize the future will help develop resilience. It gives you the motivation that drives you to learn, grow and adapt to the environment we are in. Resilience is also built up over time. If you fall, you get back up, you keep trying. You must be determined to succeed. Just like a baby that falls when they are learning to walk, if they didn't get back up they would never learn to walk.

I may have had a struggling childhood; however, I know I had positive healthy attachments growing up and I remember visualizing the future. I had a vivid imagination and acted out many stories that I believed or wanted to happen in my future. I also remember as I got older, having the motivation to achieve and learn. That amazing feeling of achieving really was like an addiction—the more I achieved, the more I wanted to try harder in order to learn and grow. One of those biggest accomplishments was when I finished my degree! From a school dropout, having a baby at sixteen years old and not being academic, I passed an Early Childhood degree! With so much determination, this paid off. And with determination, you too can accomplish anything you put your mind to and work at.

Resiliency is important as it gives you emotional strength to cope with changes or hard times that you go through in different stages of your life. If you are not resilient, you can feel overwhelmed or helpless and thinking you cannot get through the struggles. Even with resilience, you can feel like this during the times of struggle, however you will be able to keep moving, utilise your support network and work through your problems.

Most people are resilient, some are more resilient than others. At some point in our lives, we have been knocked down or defeated, however one thing I know for sure is most of us keep on going—we are still here today and we are stronger. In most cases, people who are resilient are able to recover from struggles and challenges using their problem solving skills. They are more likely able to handle stress more positively.

I was always determined growing up and going through some of my struggles, that I was going to be different. I was going change my life. Don't get me wrong, my life was not all doom and gloom—but there certainly were times I did not want my children re-living. I always had big goals for a better adult life and bigger dreams for my children. And today as I write this, I can proudly say that I have created a more improved life for myself and my three girls. I have achieved my goals. It is going through these experiences that I believe has helped me become a stronger person, able to take on hard times throughout my life, face my fears challenge myself and keep moving forward.

Don't get me wrong, I still get down, and I still go through feeling negative emotions when times get tough—I believe this is a natural process for all of us. Some struggles or changes in my life are harder than others, and some days, I face my challenges more easily than others. But with each struggle, I learn different ways to cope and different ways to feel. I know one thing for sure—I now know that having a good support system of people that I can talk to in my life helps me.

Just recently, we went to our niece's graduation and an inspirational speaker spoke—**Catriona Williams**. She had a horse riding accident and had broken her neck, resulting in her being a tetraplegic. I tell you what, she was so inspirational! She was determined to walk again so she could dance with her husband. This made me cry, and as I reflected, I thought to myself, there's always someone out there who is worse off than yourself.

She had such a great attitude and mindset, and she was determined to get back on her feet so she could dance with her husband just one more time. She was such a beautiful young lady, she seemed so happy. Yet she did say she did have bad days, and in the beginning, it was tough. A friend of her father's said to him, "Wouldn't she just be better off dead?" as she couldn't feed herself, toilet herself, pretty much nothing. At times, she thought he was right. But I guess all her resilience and her determination has helped her get through.

I just admire listening to stories like this. I think people like Catriona have every reason to be down on themselves in life, yet they are often the ones who appear so positive. They have a glowing look about them and are often energetic people!

I think we can all learn from Catriona's story. Catriona has every reason to be negative, depressed or have feelings of just hopelessness, but she somehow manages to keep a positive outlook on her life.

Really makes you look a what you have or don't have and think, "Wow! I have not been through anything like that, what am I going on about?"

Nathan Wallis, is a neuroscience educator, talks about how parents can boost their child's resilience. He believes it's important that parents model resilience themselves and take extra care on how they are responding and what they say regarding the situation that may be occurring that could be having an effect on their child. For instance, for me this was a lot of what I remember my mum doing well. For example, on the day my father arrived at our house, and we played hide and seek, my mum was careful not to show her fear to me. She was modelling resilience.

Nathan Wallis also believes that if you have trauma that happens to you as a child, you are more likely to become a negative statistic. However, you increase the chance of being okay if you have at least one positive attachment. This attachment is most important in the first 1000 days, because the first 1000 days is when the brain is developing. However, any attachment—for example, a school teacher—can have this positive influence on you.

He also says the ages of eleven to fifteen years old is not the best time for your parents to separate or for any trauma, as this is when your brain is going back to its emotional state, which he calls "gone for renovations". Nathan also says that each time you change schools or move houses, or even if you go into foster care (as he did as a young boy), this also has an effect on how you are or may turn out as an adult. He concludes that the first 1000 days of a child's life are the most important for brain development, and by the age of three, he believes you can likely tell what that child will turn out like as an adult, based on their first three years of life.

He also says in order for children to grow resilience, they need to have warm relationships built on love and trust. Children need to know when they are struggling and going through challenges that there is someone there to support them and help them process their emotions. When I attended his workshop a couple of years ago for the first time, I was absolutely amazed! I thought to myself, "Wow I have been through all these things that he was saying..."—I am a statistic!

Nathan said if your parents separate, especially when you are ten or eleven, this can have an effect on the brain. If you change schools, this too has an effect. The same goes for if you go into foster care. All these things are trauma and will have a negative effect. However, if you have at least one positive relationship with one person this increases the odds of becoming resilient.

My parents separated when I was ten. I moved houses and school constantly. And then at the age of thirteen, I was placed into foster care. It's crazy when you look at it that way. The day that I was listening to Nathan, I thought to myself, "Everything he is saying, I have been through! How then, have I turned out the way I have?" I think I had the determination to always want a better life. I had a great imagination and often imagined the life I wanted. Because of the life I'd had growing up, I knew that was a life I didn't want.

Having my husband has most certainly helped. Stu has encouraged me, believed in me and never judged me. Stu is my positive relationship that Nathan talks about. Like he says, if you have a positive relationship with one person supporting you, you can re-wire the wires in your brain.

I had known for some years that I was a statistic, but listening to it said like this in a workshop was really interesting for me. I thought, "Wow, I must have been extremely resilient." I also thought the positive relationships and having those people there for me throughout my life has made such a difference. Although I do believe too we all have choices in life, and we can either choose to be a victim to our past or upbringing or we can use our past and upbringing as a learning opportunity to help us get to where we are today.

If you are ever given the opportunity to watch Nathan at any of his workshops, I would highly recommend this. To find out more about him, I reference his website at the end of this book, you can also find him on Facebook and search YouTube for video clips.

Determination

♥

"**K**now *what you want and do not stop till you achieve—this is determination.*"

I remember as I was growing up, I would say to family members that I didn't want to be like Mum. Don't get me wrong, I love my mum, but I always wanted a better life. There was always something inside me that wanted to have a better life. I wanted to aim high. I never did well at school. I left school at the age of fifteen.

When I was fifteen, waking up one day with my best friend, I remember telling Mum we were going to go into town and get an afterschool job. Mum told me later she thought, "Oh no, I hope she doesn't get disappointed when she doesn't get one." And well... We came home that day with a job at KFC! I was determined! A similar story happened when I was nineteen; I walked into The Baby Factory and asked the manager if they had any jobs going. She said they didn't, but she took my phone number. A month or so later, she phoned me asking if I was still interested and that she had liked how friendly and bubbly I was! I got the job and worked really hard, and I enjoyed it for a couple of years—til I then got a job at Tony's Tyre Service. I have always worked really hard in all of my jobs.

When I left school and had my girls, I lost a piece of me. I lost my determination. But I always worked, and I always knew I was going to achieve something, someday. I held on to the determination, and knew I wanted a better life for my children. The partners I chose were not always great choices. I didn't really have any role models to go by. Richard really destroyed my vision and values. I looked up to other people and wanted to be like them, but he didn't want to associate with the people I wanted to associate with, so this made it very difficult. He thought they believed they were better than us and didn't want to visit them. It was funny, when I met Stu, many of his friends and family were successful business people, and I actually felt very shy and had low esteem when I met them.

I always wanted to be an ECE teacher. However, since having children so young, I had to work and needed money, so I worked in jobs such as retail. I was lucky enough to be given an amazing opportunity to work at Tony's Tyre Service in the office. This helped so much with many administration skills that I later required when my husband and I both opened our own businesses. It wasn't until I worked as an office administrator at a childcare centre when I was about twenty-seven that I thought I could get my degree in Early Childhood!

Although when I mentioned this to my husband, he said no, as he was concerned I would not finish the course and it would be a waste of money. My boss said, "No way!" and she kept pushing me and said I could do it. She was what I needed to help me stay determined!

Eventually Stu gave in and said okay. So I applied to Te Tari Puna (now Te Rito). I remember thinking, "Why would they accept me? I didn't fill out the story part right—my mind just went blank!" I had the interview, and the lady who interviewed me—who is now a very good friend of mine—was so positive and bubbly. She helped put together my case to be accepted to Te Rito. Then I had to wait to hear if I would be accepted...

A few weeks went by and waiting in anticipation felt like forever. I remember checking my emails, and I had been accepted! My mum was at my house, and I was so excited! I yelled out "I got in!" I was shaking with so much excitement. I was really doing this! I was not going to let my husband or anyone down—I was determined to pass!

Little did I know, studying with three young girls was going to be very hard! There were many late nights, many tears and arguments. My husband was amazing and would take our girls out on Sundays so I could study. I was not academic at school at all, I didn't even make it to sit school C (which is now level one). I didn't know where to begin to write an assignment—I literally just followed what I thought and starting writing. I remember the agony of waiting for the first assignment results to come back, and I passed! Every assignment I handed in, I always felt sick and always doubted that I had passed. But I always passed! I really had to have more confidence in myself, and I think it helped that I was writing about something I was passionate about.

I learnt so much about myself and what I was capable of during my time studying Early Childhood Education. I made some really great friends at my course and also at the centre I worked at. As previously mentioned, there were many late nights, tears and lots of stressful moments through-out my three years of study. But to help me stay focused and determined, I thought about something someone had once told me: "Keep your eye on the prize." So I did just this! And, I got to the end! I passed with a degree in Early Childhood Education! Such an amazing feeling, what a huge accomplishment. It was definitely worth all the sweat and tears.

Throughout my training in the centres where I did my placements, there was always something with the centre that didn't sit right with me or my philosophy—but it wasn't the centre's fault—apart from the centre I worked at; I loved that centre!

Towards the end of my study, the opportunity came up to possibly purchase this centre! So we went through the process of putting in an offer.

Unfortunately, the offer was not accepted. The thought of owning my own centre was embedded in my head now, and I was determined to open my own centre!

I had envisioned an "old school" centre, with resources that you don't see in centres today. One like a kindergarten I had attended. In the outside playground would be wooden cable reels for children to climb on, which I remember enjoying. A tyre swing. Real grass, which is something not many centres have these days. I wanted to create a environment where children felt a sense of belonging, where they were safe and happy.

So I went and saw friends I knew in the property market and told them I was looking for a property to open up my own childcare centre. We had many phone calls from agents to go and look at land with investors who would purpose build at a $100,000 lease per year and for over 100 children! Umm, thanks, but no thanks! We could not afford a big centre, especially when we were first starting out. So we continued searching.

A few weeks had passed, and I received a phone call from a friend in real estate who said a building was selling that was almost set up for a childcare centre, so I dragged Stu along to have a look! We talked, looked at the financials and then our accountant looked it over. He thought they were wanting too much for it—but me being me, I argued for it! And dug my heels in! You have to know something about me; when I want something so badly, I don't stop until I get what I want! And it's not very often I want something so badly, to be honest!

And you guessed it—the next thing I knew, we were at the doorstep of the mortgage broker, looking at our options to see if we had enough equity in our house to get the loan. Now we sat and waited. The mortgage broker came back with a few banks that had said no—one being the bank we currently banked with for many years already and who also had my husband's business for six years. Well, they didn't quite say no, they just had a list of conditions.

So it was back to the drawing board. Then the mortgage broker had a win with a bank that they don't work with, however they were in favour of lending us the money! The next thing to do was to ask my grandfather for a loan so we could set up the centre in order to get the ministry licence before the bank would lend us the money!

So I phoned up my papa and sold the idea to him. He said he would love to, but all his money was tied up in bonus bonds. You might think I would have thought, "Okay, this is the end of the road for starting my own centre..." But instead, I thought there must be a way... My papa said he would be our guarantor, but when I mentioned this to the broker, he said the bank would not accept that. Then while talking on the phone to my papa, telling him I was not able to open my own centre, he said, "Oh wait a minute, what is this?" And he found a bank statement with a significant amount of money in an account and said he could lend me the money. So we were back to buying the building!

We put in an offer and had two weeks to gather everything until it went unconditional. It was about this time that I told the centre I was working for that I would be resigning and told my boss my intentions. She tried to talk me out of starting my own centre and told me it was very stressful, as there was so much to think about. At the time, I remember thinking, no one will talk me out of this, this is my dream, this is what I want to do. This was a very stressful time.

I remember at times questioning myself, asking what am I doing? Why am I doing this? But I knew I could do it—I am resilient. My boss at the centre I worked at previously also questioned me wanting to open a centre, though she said she liked my enthusiasm. She warned me about what the biggest stresses would be. She warned me that staff was a big challenge.

They would always call in sick or leave to go to another centre. But I was passionate. And determined. This was what I wanted.

So because the bank would not give us the money for the building until we had the ministry licence, things had to be done a little bit backwards. I spent most of my evenings working on writing policies and looking at resources I could buy. The day before everything was meant to go uncon-ditional, I phoned my papa and asked him to go to the bank and get them to write a letter to say he would gift us the money.

D-day came! I remember thinking, "Oh my god, we are not going to get it!" Stu phoned me about lunch time asking if I had heard from Papa and that we only had till 4:00pm that day. I hadn't heard from him! And I said we might have to just forget it and not go through with it!

I said to him, "It's all just too much and not meant to be." I hung up and something inside me thought, just check your bank, Sharon. Knowing Papa, he might have just put the money into my account... And sure enough... There was the money we needed, sitting in my bank account! I quickly phoned Stu back to tell him what had happened...

Stu said, "Right, can you come straight down to work now to sign all the lawyer's papers?" As I went to head out the door, the phone rang and it was Papa. I so excitedly told him I got the money—but he wasn't supposed to put it in my account! He was phoning to tell me he couldn't lend me the money! He liked playing tricks on me! Papa loved playing tricks on me, but in the end, he told me he was happy he could help me out.

This was actually happening! How did I feel now? Well, I knew I had a lot of work to get through, as the part of the conditional stage was we had four weeks to prepare for the ministry and get our licence, which meant buying cots, buying resources, getting the health department in, going through the license criteria making sure I had everything, etc. Looking back now, I think, how did I know what to do, who to contact? The fire service had to be contacted for a fire scheme, B&M for the WOF, Work and Income for subsidies, APT for childcare software... And then staff...

I hadn't even decided what was I going to call this centre! I had no clue and lacked coming up with these ideas! I knew I wanted something that represented NZ and would be easy for children to remember. Stu suggested Little Ferns—and I loved it! There was heaps to think about and not much time to do this, so we did rush through it all! Looking back now, I say if you ever think about opening a centre, do not rush any of these things. Know your values, philosophy, the why—why are you doing what you are doing?

I really feel like we had to rush through all these things, as we had only four weeks to get our centre ready for licencing. One thing I think I do is rush into things—when I want something, I want it now! And I need to learn to be patient. But don't tell my husband I said this!

Over the past five years, I have owned my centre, I have learnt to be patient and not to rush—you will learn more about this throughout my book. During the time of going through the licencing stage, I was also a provisional teacher adding to my teacher registration all the time. I am not sure if this feeling is common for teachers, but I often doubted myself and didn't know what to put in my teacher registration folder. Was it enough? Was it relevant?

My mentor at the time always told me what I had was great, but I always thought, really, is she just being nice to me? But actually, I had to have faith and believe in myself! The licencing day was coming close. The week of the licencing, our family dog Jay got really sick, and my husband took him to the vet. I was so busy at the centre preparing, I told him I would pick our girls up from school and then go back to the centre, as we had the ministry coming the next day!

While I was waiting for the girls, my phone rang; it was Stu. He asked if I was going home and he said he wanted me to. I said I would take the girls home, then I asked him how Jay was. He told me he would talk to me when I got home—but I knew it was not good and I said, "No, you need to tell me." He said he had to make the call and with everything going on, he knew I had to get through this licencing stage. I did not have time to really think—it was from this moment that I had to put on a strong front, putting my feelings to the bottom and denying them. If I wanted to own my own centre, getting emotional now was not going to help.

Through this time, journaling became a weekly task for me. My advice to you if you are going through anything like this, journaling is a great way to express your emotions without bottling them up.

The next day was licensing day. My head teacher and I were ready to do this. We did well and most things were fine. There were only a few things to change. Although we didn't pass the provisional licence stage on that day, it was only a couple of days before we did. And before we knew it, we were granted provisional license and had an opening date! Things went from busy to busier as we got the license to the bank and the lawyers ready to settle. This certainly was an amazing feeling that we had finally achieved the goal I had set out to achieve. By all means, this was not an easy road, but I did not let anything or anyone's influence get in the way. Someone once told me, "We fail the minute we let someone else define success for us." And I believe that my failures made my successes so much more meaningful.

I also know that while finishing my training and wanting to open my own centre, many people talked and didn't think I could do this, but I thank these people, because it was their words that helped me be more determined not to fail. So for me, determination is hard work, not giving up or giving in until you succeed. There were certainly so many times during this process I could have easily given up and days that I thought it would be easier to give up on the idea. At the time, it felt like such a long, drawn out process, and I thought I would never achieve my dream!

But I know it was the determination that I was not going to fail that helped me succeed. I saw a goal, I had a vision that I was going to own a centre, and I was not going to stop till that vision became a reality. I heard from some of my close friends that there was talk that I wasn't going to be able to start a childcare centre. I guess this gave me the determination to prove them wrong. I knew there had to be a way. I had visualised owning my own centre. I would find a way.

What I am trying to say to you is that if you have dream and you think you will never be able to achieve it, you won't. If you believe in yourself and your dream you will succeed. There are ways, and you can have a dream, talk about it, visualise it and you will make it a reality like I did.

Have you ever wanted something so bad yet had people say that it's impossible or there's no way what you want will ever happen? Well for me—and it's weird, and I cannot explain it—but when this has happened to me, it has only made me more determined to achieve or succeed. Maybe scenarios like these have an influence on your chances of achieving your dream or not?

How do I achieve the things I want in life, you may ask. Well, let me offer you some ideas and tools to help you on this journey.

We all dream, right? Who hasn't sat around, talking with their friends about what they would spend the money on if they won the lotto? I've often had these conversations, and I decided that if I won the lotto, I would go on a family holiday. Even if we don't win the lotto, this is how our dream begins—sitting around the table, having conversations with our friends or family about the dreams that we have. Sometimes these dreams become more serious ideas. We continue to think about these dreams and wonder how we can make them happen.

My suggestion is to first write down your dreams, your ideas. Be specific about what it looks like. Write about it as if you are already living in that life. If you want to buy a dog, ask yourself what kind of dog do you have, what is its personality? Be as specific as you can.

Grab your journal, if you don't have a journal yet, now may be a great time to get one. When writing in your journal, always write down the date. So you can go back and relook at it in months, years to come.

In your journal write down your dreams, focus on the first dream that you want to achieve the most, or the one you think will be most achievable. No dream is silly, too big or too small.

Write your dream down in a goal form. I suggest writing your goal using the **SMART** goal method. The **SMART** goal is a great tool to use to increase your chance of achieving your goal.

SMART goals are:

Specific: State exactly what you aim to do.

Measurable: How you will measure your progress, how often? how many?

Achievable: Just know and believe it is achieveable

Realistic: Set reasonable expectations for achieving your goal

Timely: Establish a timeframe for achieving your goal

Next share your dream, your idea with someone you trust, be that your mum, dad, partner or friend. Saying our dreams out loud makes the dream seem more real. And if you are serious about this dream, sharing your idea is also making you accountable. And each time we share stories, we imagine. And when you imagine and visualise what you want as if you have it, you will hold onto this feeling and the determination to succeed.

An example of my goal would be:

January 6th 2023

My goal is to run 10ks without stopping. In order to achieve this goal, I will use the running app on my phone each week for eight weeks. The goal will be achieved by the end of March.

What Success Means to Me

♥

"*Success is working hard, believing in yourself and never giving up.*"

As a young child, I remember always thinking I wanted to be successful. I wanted to make my family proud. I wanted to make a difference and I wanted to help people. I didn't know how I would get there, but that was what I wanted.

Through all of my school years, I don't remember a time that I was successful. I always made friends, but we moved so often that I did not keep those friends for very long. I struggled with the school work, and I always struggled with the teachers, as I was never at the same school long enough to form a relationship with them.

I remember probably the very first time I felt successful was the day I woke up and told my mum my best friend and I were going to get a job. I think I was about fifteen. We went on our way, got an interview at KFC and both of us got the job! When I went home that afternoon, I was really excited to tell my mum I had got a job at KFC.

Later in life, my mum told me she felt so worried that I had this positive mindset and I had told her I was getting a job. She didn't want me to be disappointed that I couldn't just get a job like that. But she didn't need to worry—I was successful! How? Well, even I don't know that. I guess it was due to my positive mindset and because I had already envisioned that I would be working. I stayed at my job for two years, after leaving school and having my first daughter.

A few years went by, and this was where I hit rock bottom. I was probably successful at many more things during these years, but I have not put too much thought into these years.

I remember buying my very first nice car! I borrowed a couple of thousand dollars off my papa. I was proud and successful when I paid all the money back to him.

Then finishing my degree in ECE was a very important achievement for me, and I think this was a major success for me. I was the first in my family to receive a degree.

For me, achieving life's milestones that I was destined not to achieve has been a way of measuring success for me. Getting married to my husband and remaining married to him for coming up on nine years is success to me, as well as having my three girls and being the best mum I was and still am with the best I know how.

But my success has not been easy at all. I have always had to work hard, and I am sure I will always work hard in order to achieve the things I want to in life.

As previously mentioned, a few years ago, I went to a workshop run by Nathan Wallis. It was at this workshop that I realised I was a statistic, destined to fail. However without having experiencing the life I have had, I believe I would not have the life I have today. I would love to study psychology and look into this more someday. Maybe I can then write another book!

Now as an adult, I see success as many things. Remaining happily married to my husband is a huge success. So is having and being proud of all three of my girls and their achievements, supporting my husband when we opened his business, setting up all the systems and encouraging and convincing him that we could do it. That was a massive accomplishment. So was starting my own business, and many more successes I have experienced in life. I believe success is a forever evolving thing. It's not just having money—in fact, we don't have money and I feel as though being successful comes from what we do and the way we are within, who we are.

Over the five years I had owned my centre, I had so many staff come and go. I had learnt so much by asking myself how am I managing staff, what is wrong with the way I am doing things? I went straight from study to opening my own childcare centre! This was a crazy thought! And one that I didn't really think through. Many people might have thought I would fail for sure. I mean, how can someone go straight out of study to start up their own business, managing staff and a whole business?

There have certainly been many ups and downs, and I have learnt a whole heap. At the time of writing this book (2020), I had been considering selling my centre, as this year has been a real struggle with Covid. More and more centres are getting built all over the place, and teachers are getting harder to come by. I have recently had a teacher resign, leaving me to advertise for a new one, but we have had no applications for this.

Every day I wake up, and the first thing I do is look at my cell phone to see which team member is calling in sick. Today I was sick, and I did not want to look at my cell phone, I did not want anyone to call in sick! But this morning, it happened again! A team member called in sick! And to top it all off, it was my only qualified team member. Being a business owner, you suck it up. You have to. You get your sad arse out of bed and get to work! My daughter also came to stay from Dunedin and asked why I don't just get more staff. Mmm, well... if only it were this easy, right?

So today I got up and I went to work, as I always do. Yes, at times I felt sorry for myself, and my throat was sore! My daughter told me I shouldn't have been going to work—but what choice did I have?

Why can't I call in sick? Why can I not just have a day at home because I am not feeling up to it? All you business owners out there will know that calling in sick is a very seldom thing you do, and you only do it when you are actually sick and not able to get out of bed! Every manager or owner knows a leader comes last. It takes a strong person to be a leader, yet why do we all want to be leaders?

What research says about success

Everyone has different ideas about what success looks like for them. Bob Proctor believes that success is about making a decision that you are going to get there. I know I am here and I want to get *there*. I don't know how I will get there but I *am* going to get there. Sir Edmond Hillary climbed mount Everest; however, he failed two times before he eventually succeeded. He shows us that if you stay focused and are persistent that you can achieve your goals—this is success. From those I interviewed, they have all said similar things about what success looks like to them. What does success look like to you? Have a think about it, dig deep. If you have been writing in your journal, write what success means to you in there.

Later in my book, I go through an exercise with you to look at your achievements—I am sure you will be surprised.

John Wooden defines success as "peace of mind, which is a direct result of self-satisfaction in knowing you made the effort to do your best to become the best that you are capable of becoming."

The first step of success is first defining success for yourself, knowing where you want to go. You will have setbacks and failures along the way, and you may not know how long it will take you to get to the end result you want. You are successful as long as you know where you are going and remain persistent.

So how come sometimes we don't always achieve our goals? Is this because we are not persistent? Do some have more drive to succeed then others?

I have had friends before who have said to me, "Sharon, you are so lucky you have Stu."—or a house, or whatever it may be. Well, let me tell you, luck has nothing to do with it. I have goals, I know what I want to achieve in life, and most of the time I stay focused. Sometimes I fail at what I set out to do, but I keep trying. I keep going, and nine times out of ten, I do not stop until I achieve what I set out to – this is success. I have worked hard for years and years to get to where I am today. I have come up against challenges, fighting my way through them.

Life is a funny thing. Looking at other people's lives, they look like they have it all, and often if they have something we want but we don't have, we think how lucky they are. But we too could be that lucky! We just have to work hard like they did. We don't always see or appreciate the hard work that others put into their lives. We just see them as having a great life and being lucky. But I assure you, luck does not have anything to do with what you get or have in life. Making the right choices, working hard and time is what gets you to be where you see your friends or family.

Success should not be determined by the approval or recognition of others. You are the one who holds the key to your own success and choose the road you plan to travel. However, you can ask for help along the way. Success is knowing when to ask for help and that it is okay to ask for help. In no way are you a failure if you have to ask for help. For some of us, we really struggle to ask for help. I am one of those people. Even when I am struggling and a friend offers help, I turn it down. Even though deep down I would like to take it. I don't want to be a burden on others. There have been times though that I would not have succeeded had I had not had help from my friends or family.

Success also comes from believing in yourself. Dr James Doty's book, "Into the Magic Shop", which I highly recommend, talks about believing in yourself. He suggests closing your eyes and imagining that you already have what it is you want to achieve. "You can have anything you want by visualizing that it's already yours. It's that simple and hard at the same time." Have you ever been for a job interview and really visualized yourself working there, even imagining where you would sit? And then you got the job! Or maybe there's a job you might not be able to visualize working at, and you don't get the job? I have practiced visualizing before and have been successful at what I visualized.

As a young child of about maybe four or five years old, I remember my mum taking me to the skating rink. I couldn't skate and I kept falling over. I told her I couldn't do it. My mum said to me to say over and over "I can skate, I can skate" and to imagine I could skate. I did this, and I remember being so excited at that very moment after trying so hard that I did it! I skated from one side of the wall to the other (slowly) on my own! This is what I think defines success.

Yes, I did fail and I fell over quite a few times—but I did not let this stop me from continuing to get back up and try again. I remember it being hard at the time and thinking, why can I not do this? But there was also something inside me that said, "Sharon, you can do this, you just have to keep getting back up and trying."

Each time I fell on my butt, it hurt! And I certainly fell a lot of times that day. But I also got back up with the help of my mum and kept on trying, until eventually I did not fall down! That feeling inside me of achieving made me so excited. I wanted to scream to the world that I did it. My heart was racing with excitement. However, if I hadn't had my mum there to encourage me and support me, I do not know if I would have wanted to keep getting back up.

Does the encouragement from others help us with the determination to be successful? I think it most certainly does. For example, writing this book—at times I have really felt like it is so hard. I just can't do it anymore. However, I have told too many of my friends and family about it, and they are always asking me how is it going. It's their encouragement that I think of which helps me keep going. I have come too far in this journey to stop here. I am and I will succeed in writing and finishing this book!

I believe in order to be succeed, you first need to see yourself as someone who is capable of learning. And in order to succeed, you also must be willing to fail. Failure is a lesson for me. At times I have failed, and I have thought to myself, I do not want to fail. This is not an option. So, I persevere. Like I have said previously, I find if I have discussed what it is I am setting out to achieve, then I want to achieve it more then ever. So, I keep trying. I find ways to achieve.

Sometimes you may not always achieve your goals. For example, if you go for a job interview and you want that job so much, but you don't get it. You feel as though you failed. You feel let down. Yes, it can be so disappointing when you get rejected. The piece of advice I would have for you is not to let that stop you from continuing to apply for other jobs. Research on the internet or in books what makes a good job interview. Talk to your friends about what they said at their job interviews. Keep going, keep persevering.

Do not take failure personally. Failing means you should get back up and try again. Remain positive and keep your eye on the prize, the end goal, and keep with your vision. Some falls are harder than others, and you think to yourself, how on earth am I going to get there? Trust me, there have been many times that I've fallen, and I could have easily given up. I have had others put me down or talk behind my back and thought I would most likely fall. And yes, falling bloody hurts! It sucks down at the bottom while everyone else is up at the top, and that's why if you do find yourself as the bottom, you don't want to stay there for too long. You'll be missing out on all the fun at the top!

Earlier this year, we did the Tongariro Crossing, and it was damn hard! The Tongariro Crossing is a beautiful volcanic mountain. The hike is 19.4 kms and you climb 3923 feet high! It takes six to eight hours to walk.

The first part of the walk was so exciting, then up the first set of stairs was okay. But as you got higher, it got harder. At the second set of stairs, I started to struggle—but we did it. We walked along a bit of flat and then uh oh, in the distance we could see more stairs!

I thought again to myself, this is crazy. But I also thought, Sharon, you have to do this; you cannot go back because either way, you have lots of stairs to climb. We just had to stop a few times as the higher up we got I started to feel lightheaded, especially right up at the top. We continued, and we did it! This is success. We set out with the goal in mind that we were going to walk the Tongariro Crossing. And we achieved it. We did it.

Along the way, a helicopter came and picked up a young girl who was not looking so good, and I thought to myself she must be so disappointed. However, I bet she will attempt to do it again, if her goal was to achieve this.

Harvard Business review business expert Erika Andersen is the founding partner of Proteus, a coaching, consulting, and training firm that focuses on leader readiness. Erika says on her website, there are "four mental tools we can use to help ourselves changing or starting a new challenge, these compose of: **Aspiration:** Picturing how good it will feel to achieve our goals, we are more likely to be motivated to work on this. **Self-awareness:** Thinking about your strengths and weaknesses and how can you continue to grow and develop. **Curiosity:** Keep on learning, we are all born to continue to learn, gain new knowledge and new experiences. **Vulnerability:** Staying in your comfort zone, sounds like a great idea doesn't it? However, this is no way to improve. In order to learn new things, we must step outside our comfort zone, make mistakes along the way and learn from them."

In my lifetime, I have used each of these tools in some way. Stepping outside our comfort zone is one of the hardest things for most people to do, isn't it? I know for me there are times I have struggled with doing certain things that are outside my comfort zone. But for me, it's either I do these things and gain more knowledge, learning new things, or I stay in the same place year after year and don't gain anything. I know which one I prefer.

A couple of years ago, I hosted a conference with international speaker Anthony Semann talking for ECE teachers. I had to intoduce him, get up and speak in front of eighty people. Speaking in front of five people, let alone eighty, was hard for me! This was definitely getting out of my comfort zone! I was so nervous; I remember I had a V (an energy drink) and then some rescue remedy (which is supposed to calm your nerves)—even though each contradicted the other!

I had organised this day, and I had no choice but to get up on that stage and talk! Sometimes you just have to get in there and do it without giving yourself too much time to think. Anyway, I was actually really proud of myself that day. One of my staff recorded me, and at first I thought, I can't watch it, I will sound terrible. But I was so surprised at how well I did, and I was actually clear enough for the eighty people to hear me! The achievement I felt just knowing this was far out of my comfort zone was amazing! I even had people I didn't know coming up to me afterwards saying I did such a great job. They probably felt sorry for me and could see how nervous I was.

Who Influences You and Why It's Important

♥

"*Choose those you spend your time with wisely, those that influence you in a good way*"

Consider this—if you want to be successful, surround yourself with successful people. If you want to be healthy and fit, surround yourself with healthy and fit people. I believe that we are like the people who we hang out with. For example, Nicholas Christakis' research shows that non-drinkers who spend time with people who drink significantly increase their chance of becoming drinkers themselves.

My business mentor, Sarah Greener, talks about how your friends have a 35% influence over you, their friends have a 15% influence on you, and friends of friends of friends who you don't even know or have never met have a 5% influence on you! That's so crazy, right? If you surround yourself with wise people, it is contagious, and you will be wise. What you do today, and think about today will influence who you are tomorrow.

However, we are in control of our feelings and the things that we do! For example, we can choose to go to work or to be our very best. What you choose to do in life might feel right for you and not be the influence of others. You are in control of your destiny—it is not your mother, father, or friend's fault. You choose to do everything, so choose what you do or don't do wisely.

What I am not saying here is that how you are treated by your parents or friends is your fault. You are in control of how you respond. I love what author **Rhonda Byrne** says in her book, "The Secret to Love, Health and Money": "Remember, life isn't happening to you; life if responding to you. Life is your call! Whether you want a perfect partner, a better marriage, or a better relationship with your boss, simply get yourself onto the receiving frequency." Ronda guides us to imagine and feel what it would be like to have that relationship. In order to attract the relationship you want, imagine that relationship exactly how you want it to be.

I find this so interesting because when I was a young teen, I did in fact attract boys that were not so good for me. I mean these two relationships weren't terrible, they just weren't what I had envisioned my relationships to be like. I guess that's all I thought I was worth. In her book, Rhonda talks about how when you are in negative relationships, you tend to use their imagination and talk about all the things they don't want. I found myself doing this all the time. I remember thinking I don't want to be in a relationship where my partner smokes or spends all his time in his shed. I didn't want a partner who looked at other girls. So all I was doing was focusing all my thoughts on what I didn't want. And this is.... What I got!

Especially with my second long-term relationship, since I really believed I deserved everything I got with him. It wasn't until I thought long and hard that I realized I needed to surround myself with people who I wanted to be like. Don't get me wrong—I love this guy dearly, and we will always be great mates; he is the father of my daughter, and today, we do get on well. Beginning my job at Tony's Tyre Service was the start of where I began to change my mindset and started thinking positively.

My youngest daughter struggled all through primary and intermediate, however when she went to high school, she met some really lovely friends who all helped each other to succeed, and my daughter began to understand learning. She has just this week told me she got into the highest maths class for next year! And I know there are two reasons for this; firstly, she has surrounded herself with friends that want to learn and try really hard, and secondly, my daughter had her goal in mind and worked hard to achieve that goal. We become the people we hang out with. If we are friends with negative people who like to gossip, it is likely we will be like this too, and we will find most of the people we know will be similar.

Reading and following inspirational people on social media can also help, and this helped me. The important message I am trying to give you here is to be familiar with what influence your friends are having on you. Ask yourself, are they good influences or bad influences? For the ones who are poor influences, you don't have to stop being friends with them at all—just try to spend more time with those who are great influences or who you find inspirational. For me, I know I enjoy spending time with my family and friends who share common interests, or who I aspire to be like and I know I want to learn from.

Friends help you up when you are down, they help motivate you and friends can give you great advice or not so great advice—which will have an impact or influence on the choices you make on a regular basis. It is said that you become like those who you surround yourself with. For example, if you want to be happy, surround yourself with happy people.

Facebook, or any social media platforms, can have a major effect on us all in regard to our influences. You may have different friends on your Facebook page, some are positive and some negative. They all have an effect and an influence over you. For example, if you have a friend who constantly posts negative posts, you may not take too much notice to these on a daily basis—however, if you are having a bad day, you are likely to read this post and it will get you down somewhat more.

If you have friends in your life or even on your Facebook page who are not adding value to your life positively, you might want to reconsider how much time you spend with them or not watching their page. I have recently gone through this process of eliminating people from my Facebook and really focusing on the inspirational people I want in my life. In the next chapter, I will tell you a small handful of the people who have and still influence me today.

My Influences

♥

*"**W**ho has influenced and motivated me and I aspire to be like"*

Throughout each stage and age of my life, many different people have influenced me, some in a negative way and some positively. In this chapter, I will talk about the main people who have influenced me or motivated me throughout different times in my life. We all have different people come and go from our lives, some have positive effects and some negative. I am only going to talk about the handful of those who inspired me and had positive effects on my life. There are many more who have influenced me and still continue to influence me today. Some days, the lady on the checkout who smiles at me influences me. But in this chapter, I am just focusing on the main influences in my life.

Probably my very first inspirational person is definitely my papa. From the age of three, I remember spending all my time with him, and I remember the memories of him were always positive. My papa taught me to believe in myself, how to save money, and to have principles and stick to them. As a young child, I remember he used to play tricks on me and he enjoyed teasing me. My papa was my idol. I was his biggest fan right up until the day he passed away—and I still look up to the life experiences he taught me and remember the amazing man he was.

When I think about my Childcare centre and when I am struggling with things, I always go think about my papa. I am doing this for him, he would be so proud of me and the centre! This keeps me strong, and I know how proud Papa would be today if he were still alive. Papa and I would talk every week, and if he phoned and I wasn't home, I was so upset as I had missed our phone call. He phoned me and my girls on our birthdays every year without fail, and we always got $10 from him on our birthdays. And then he kindly loaned me money to help me open the centre! I will be forever grateful, and I was so proud when I paid it all back. I was just disappointed that he was not alive to celebrate the success with me. But inside, I knew he would be proud and is always looking over me.

Another person who influenced me was one of my teachers at primary school, Mr Watson. I had got into the finals at the school cross country. Mr Watson dedicated his afterschool hours to help train me as he could see the potential I had and knew I could achieve interschool. I remember him cheering me on, telling me I could do it. He spent each day after school, on his own time, to help train me. Unfortunately, on the morning of, I had a asthma attack and could not make it to compete the interschool! I remember being so disappointed, and for some reason, throughout my life this happened a lot when I got excited about something!

Then there's a friend of mine who I went to high school with; her mum was and still is a great inspirational person I am influenced by. Let's call her Kate. She has raised four beautiful girls, and she is still successfully and happily married to her husband of forty-seven years! That on its own is an inspiration for me. As a teenager then and now today, I still have so much respect for Kate. I always admired the amazing mum she is and thought if I was half the mum that Kate is, I would be a great mum.

Kate did not have her own mum there for her when she was growing up, so she did not have a role model for how to parent her children. But

I honestly can say, she has done such an amazing job, and with her girls all now grown up, all but married and with children, they are a really close-knit family—something I admire as that's not what I had at all growing up. So for me, spending time with this family was and is still very important. Again, I feel drawn to surround myself with this family and I enjoy spending my time with them. Kate has also always made me feel a part of her family, she has never judged me and always been there for me.

Throughout my Early Childhood studies, there were many influences who really helped motivate me, they helped shape the teacher I am today—especially my boss and her daughter at the first centre I worked at during my study.

Then there are the mentors I had, especially Pania, who helped me and supported me through my te ao Māori education. She always believed in me. When things would get tough for me, she would remind me why I was doing what I was doing, and that was for my Papa. She was always there for me, trying to cheer me up and help me see the positive side of life. Pania always says to me I overthink too much, or I analyse everything. She knows me so well and has always been there for me when I have been in some dark times.

Steve Lange and Tony's Tyre Service had a massive influence over my life. It was here that the beginning of my journey to a positive mental attitude began. This is where I began to change my thinking, as we were not allowed to say the word 'good' and if we did, we had to do five step-ups. I was the receptionist, and I remember answering the phone with "It's a great day," or "It's a fantastic day at Tony's Tyre Service." And after doing it so many times during the day, I actually began to feel fantastic—not to mention the reactions of the people on the other end of the phone. And most told me I had made their day!

I remember one thing Steve said once that has always really stuck in my mind. "You spend 80% of your life working, so you might as well be working at what you enjoy." Working at Tony's Tyre Service really changed my life, my confidence really grew and I began to feel great about myself. It was here that I began to regain my vision of what I wanted in life.

And then there's my husband, but shhh, don't tell him that I said he has influenced me! When we met, I was just around twenty-three. We worked togeth." at the Support Centre for a year and a bit before we became an "item". Stu helped me figure out a few things about myself and how only I could make myself happy. I really enjoyed his company, but I never thought of it as anything more. He was just a really nice guy with so much advice. Those that know my husband know that he is a very positive, friendly person with so much energy all the time. I remember when I first met him thinking, how can this guy be happy all the time! Surely he must be on something to make him so alive all the time, but no. He was (and still is) happy.

Tony's Tyre Service had also had a massive influence on him too. As I know a lot of other people who worked there have said the same.

In the seventeen years that Stu and I have been together, not much stops Stu from working. Even when he snapped his Achilles, he still drove and went to work—even though he shouldn't have!

Remember I said earlier there is a sixteen-year age difference. I was twenty-four and he was forty! I remember at the time thinking, oh shit! What? Ummm, this cannot happen! How will I tell anyone, and what will all my friends and family think or say? I know many people had reservations about us and didn't think it would work. And to be honest, they had every reason to have thought this! In the end, it did not matter, I had an enormous amount of respect for this guy and he treated me like a princess.

And what we had and still have works really well. We are both happy and complement each other well.

At the time of us meeting, Stu was raising his ex-partner's twelve-year-old daughter by himself—this alone showed me what an amazing, empathetic guy he was. Now, seventeen years on, and I can say it still feels like just the other day we met. He is still the fun, positive, high-energy man I met all those years ago and that was what I admire about him. Whenever I have been down or have gone through struggles in my life, he has always encouraged me and told me he is proud of all that I have achieved. I enjoy talking with Stu about any issues or anything in general, as he always has a different look on things than I do, and more often than not, he is right—although my papa would joke and say he was always wrong! This was a little joke my papa had just before he passed away. Although I know papa thought the world of Stu as well.

Summing up all those who have influenced me so far in my life, and there have been others that have influenced me and I am currently inspired to be like, without these people I would not have become the person I am today. I have many friends who today influence me and I aspire to be like. I like to surround myself with these people as much as I can. I also like to have an influence on my friends and be there for them, giving them advice when they need it as well.

It has been important to me, and it will be important for you to ensure you have people in your life that you can look up to and be inspired to be like. In my next chapter, I go more into talking about how people have an impact and an influence over you, sometimes even those people that you don't know. So it's important that you know what sort of person you want to be so you can be purposeful about choosing the influences that are around you all the time.

Often there were times in my life when I have come across someone or have been introduced to someone and I have thought I'd really like to get to know that person, it would be so great if I could befriend them. I have admired them. And then before I know it, I have been introduced to them and become friends with them. I have been so amazed at the fact that what I put out into the universe has come into fruition! It's always good to have people to look up to, be inspired by, and want to be like or learn from.

You can learn so much from people who have been through similar situations as you or just people who you can see are at stages of their life that you want to reach. This happened to me recently with a good friend of mine. Earlier in the year, another friend of mine mentioned her and said we would be great friends and support for each other as she also owns a childcare centre.

I was so excited and nervous when my friend introduced us. It's funny, I really wanted to be introduced, and then when we did get introduced, I was nervous. Sometimes I struggle to talk with people who are so much more successful than I am. I know, you are probably saying this is a subconscious thing, and in my next chapter, I will talk about the subconscious and the conscious mind. Because often, especially as women, we tend to overthink everything. We get inside our own head and make up stories and we overthink things like, what should I wear? How do I stand? But in all honesty, we should just be ourselves!

Subconscious and Conscious Mind

♥

"You are what you think you are. Think wisely"
The next part of what helped me was learning about the conscious and subconscious mind. When I was working with my business coach, **Sarah Greener**, she explained to me that 85% of the thoughts we have are negative! And 90% of thoughts are repetitive. Your thoughts become your story. What you put out into the universe, you will get back.

So, I started asking myself, what am I thinking and feeling on a daily basis? What do I want to believe? What do I want to believe and feel until I become it? You are responsible for everything in your life. You cannot control what others do or say, but you can control how you respond to situations. Jocko Williams and Leif Babin talk about taking extreme ownership—owning everything in your world, meaning you are responsible for not just the tasks which you can control, but also for those that affect whether or not you are successful at what you are doing.

Reflecting on many things going on in my life, I realised I was not taking ownership. I often blamed other people, and up until very recently, I always blamed others for situations that would or wouldn't work out. Your subconscious mind does not understand jokes or any thoughts as negative or positive. It takes everything literally and when repeated frequently new habit is formed. If you talk about other people negatively, your subconscious thinks you are talking about yourself, and it believes you. So, I learnt to be crystal clear about what it is I want. I am now deliberate in my language, and I think and speak more positively, and I write down the things I want.

Think of your conscious mind as a magnet. You will attract what you spend the most time focusing on. If you focus on what you don't want, you will get more of those things. If I was to tell you not to think of a blue car, what are you doing right now? I bet you are thinking of a blue car! Your mind does not understand "don't" or "not". Your mind is literal. You need to be specific with what you want and what you wish for.

If you wake up in the morning and the first thing you think is, "Oh damn it, today is going to be a hard day." Well, guess what? You will get a hard day, and then you will be disappointed and feel angry, right? Interesting, isn't it? So, I began this new journey! I told myself and wrote down all the things I am and what I already have, and interestingly, my friends began commenting on the qualities I was focusing on!

Just recently, I saw a friend I haven't seen for months, and she said to me, "Sharon, you are looking so confident!" I didn't tell her that I had been working on that quality! But I was thinking, "Yuss, this is working!" And trust me, it truly does work.

Another book I had been reading on developing intuition says, "We cannot create what we cannot imagine, yet we always create what we do imagine." Our thoughts create our lives—we have control over our thoughts, we just need to replace the negative thoughts with positive thoughts and begin to imagine those thoughts. I began making small changes, writing my story about who I wanted to be and what I believe about myself to be true.

Little by little, making small changes and each day, I began to feel in control and positive about my feelings and how I was showing up. I also believe **Louise Hayes**, who says, "Whatever you believe becomes true for us." You are in control of your thoughts, your mind, but again, you are the only person who can change your thoughts. If you think and act happy or enthusiastic, you will feel happy and enthusiastic. If you think you can, you can. If you think you can't, you are right.

The subconscious mind obeys everything from the conscious mind, which is the commander. Therefore, your subconscious is such a powerful tool. A great exercise that I recently began doing is writing down, visualizing and acting my goals or desires as if I already have them and how I already am showing up. Visualize your goal, but visualize this as if you already have achieved it.

For instance, if you want a new house or car, visualize yourself as clear as you can in that car, including what colour is it, what you are wearing in the car, and see yourself driving in it. Do this on a daily basis or write it down and read it out loud. Write down the attributes you are—for instance, I am confident, I am clear and happy.

I made up a poster of pictures of my family, friends, books and the things that are important to me in my life. I then wrote down all the things that I already am. I have attached this at the end of the book for you to read, I have this up on my fridge to remind myself of what I am. I intend to change this regularly, as change and move forward in life.

How I Lost My Values

♥

"*A* lways stay true to your values"
I always knew I wanted to make a difference, I wanted to help parents and children that were not so fortunate. I wanted to have a positive impact on families. I had dreamt of my centre, and I had pictured the way I wanted it—with natural resources and as homely as possible. I wanted to create positive memories for the children like I had growing up as a child. I remember the big cable wooden reels, tyre swing, play dough and all the yummy party food at birthdays!

Making a difference is my top value. Making the most of time and relationships are also very important values to me.

On opening my centre, finances were tight—and time was also limited, so I could not purchase all the resources I would have liked. However, I did get the cable reel, and I did have the real grass! So, this was a bonus. It was hard to keep to my values for some things, as when I began employing teachers they too came with their own values and ideas, and slowly, we began to change some of the ideas at the centre. I allowed others at times to slowly change my ideas for the centre, but at the time, I had doubt in myself and I thought it was okay to do this. In some cases, the values were only small and not so significant.

However, one value I was extremely passionate about was having karakia every single day. Karakia is a Māori term for saying a prayer or giving thanks for the day. This is something the centre started with, and I had never envisioned it would not have karakia. The team at this time had said karakia was a stressful time, and they did not want to do it. It just wasn't worth it for them, so I allowed this. After talking with my husband about this, he reminded me of my values and how important this was for me.

So I did in fact say to the team that we would go back to doing karakia and maybe we could look at the reasons why it wasn't working.

I very quickly forgot what my values were. I wanted to please everyone, but this was proving to be really hard. **Brene Brown**, who is an American professor, lecturer, author, and podcast host, is known in particular for her research on shame, vulnerability, and leadership, and for her widely viewed TEDx talk. I became a fan of Brene's and started reading her books on vulnerability and leadership.

Brene defines values as "a way of being and believing that we hold most important. Living into our values means that we do more than profess our values, we practice them. We walk our talk—we are clear about what we believe and hold important, and we take care that our intentions, words, thoughts and behaviours align with those beliefs." What I learnt from this experience was that I had let myself down, I was not being true to my values. However, it wasn't until this moment that I realised how important this value was for me.

Mark Manson, who wrote "The Subtle Art of Not Giving a F**k" says, "Values are won and lost through life experiences." I had to go through this experience in order to learn how important this value really was to me, and I will be sticking to this value. In this situation, I now know I was responsible for how this went. I cannot blame the teachers for not wanting karakia. I chose how to respond to their wants, and I am sure if I had to do it all over again, it would probably be the same result, as I believe I had to go through that process to understand and experience how important my value was to me.

Another story of losing sight of my values happened before I opened my centre. I would ALWAYS be super early to appointments, or for dropping the girls off at school, picking them up; anywhere I had to go, I would always be early without fail. This is a value that has been handed down to me from my papa, he would always tell me to always leave home 20 minutes before I had to be anywhere in case something were to happen. You never knew, there could be road works on the road or a car accident. Sometimes I would be super early—and this was an embarrassment! But in hindsight, I would rather be early than late.

Anyway, after opening my centre and working on the floor with the children, I would make appointments or times for meetings, but things would come up, parents would turn up to talk with me, or the phone would ring and I could not get to the appointment on time. In the beginning, I would get bad anxiety and panic, but as time went on and it became more regular, I had to accept this was not in my control and that I could not be fully responsible for being late if it was because of someone else who needed my attention as well. I learnt it was my response to this, and accepting helped with the way I dealt with it and I began to feel better. Don't get me wrong, it is still my value to be early when I need to be somewhere, and I still do make every effort to be early. I'm just not so hard on myself when it's out of my control and I am either on time or late.

I have learnt through all of these experiences that I have been faced with many different challenges within my personal life and work life. At times, my responses were negative and my reactions were not carefully thought through. One thing I know for sure is your values are your values. You should not let anyone talk you into changing your values or beliefs.

Your values can change over months, years—absolutely. As you grow and change, so do your thoughts, right? You may change your values.

Values are a great measure of how we are living, not in terms of right or wrong, but whether how we are feeling is in alignment with the way we act. Think about what you want in life, the person you are, who you want to be. What do you believe in so strongly?

If you are unsure of what your values are, I challenge you to do the following exercise. Please note this exercise has been put together from the knowledge of author Brene Brown. This is not my work. I have taken it and adjusted to suit. If you get the chance to look more into her work, Brene has lots of great books, podcasts and resources out there.

Brene Brown says that our values should be clear in our minds. They are not a value by choice—they are a definition of who we are in our lives.

Here are a list of words that you may associate with values. I want you to look at the list and decide on the values that resonate with you. Write down up to ten values you resonate with. Then when you have your ten, I want you to look at this list, deeper. Ask yourself the following questions about each value you have chosen.

Does this define me?

Is this who I am at my best?

Is this a filter that I use to make hard decisions?

If the answer is no, then cross out that value from your list until there are only two values left.

For the next step of this exercise, you need two values that resonate strongly with you. This is often a really hard exercise to do.

For each value, ask yourself these questions:

What are one or two behaviours that support your value?

What is an example when you were fully living into this value?

Who is someone who knows your values and supports your efforts to live into them?

What does support look like from this person?

What does it feel like when you are living into your values?

What does it feel like when you are not living into your values?

List of values

Accountability Fairness JoySelf-expression

Achievement Faith Justice Self-respect

Adaptability Family Kindness Service

Adventure Financial Stability Knowledge Simplicity

Ambition Forgiveness Leadership Spirituality

Authenticity Freedom Learning Success

Balance Friendship Legacy Teamwork

Beauty Fun Leisure Time

Being the Best Future generations Love Tradition

Belonging Boundaries Generosity Loyalty Travel

Career Giving back Making a Difference Trust

Caring Grace Nature Truth

Collaboration Gratitude Openness Understanding

Commitment Growth Order Uniqueness

Community Harmony Parenting Usefulness

Confidence Health Patience Vision

Connection Home Peace Vulnerability

Contentment Honesty Perseverance Wealth

Contribution Hope Personal Fulfilment Well-being

Cooperation Humility Power Wholeheartedness

Courage Humour Pride Wisdom

Creativity Inclusion Recognition

Dignity Independence Respect

Environment Initiative Responsibilities
Efficiency Integrity Risk taking
Equality Excellence Intuition Joy Safety
Ethics Job security Security Self-discipline

Here are three of the values that I hold dear to me:

- Making a Difference

- Security

- Responsibility

I remember when I first started looking at my values, I really struggled. I could easily tell you what my husband's values were, but if you had asked me what mine were, I would say to you, "What? My values? I am not even sure I have any values." I know all the values I would like to uphold, but I struggle to do so.

I know I am fully living into my values of security, and providing security and consistency for my girls. This would be my highest value of all. Responsibility is a value that had been given to me at a young age, but I definitely value being responsible. And then making a difference is high up there as well; I love to know that I am helping others and making a difference.

Overcoming a Storm

♥

"**S**torms, will come and go—sometimes they change direction. Are you prepared?"

In life, there will always be ups and downs, waves will come crashing in when we least expect it. Being prepared for the next storm is something I had never thought of. In fact, I still don't know if I would ever be fully prepared for another storm. Each storm that comes our way is always going to be different, and we won't always be able to control how the storm ends up, but we can control how we are showing up and feeling during the storm.

I also believe if you wait and ecpect for storms or negative moments in your life, this will happen. The mind is a powerful tool and you can create the stories in your life.

In March 2021, I hit rock bottom. I was in a very dark place and was not sure if I could climb to the top. But something inside me—resilience, possibly—had to keep going. Giving up was never an option. I just had to learn how to control how I was showing up and feeling. Through every storm, there is always a lesson that we can learn from. Falling down and getting back up only makes you stronger. The storm does eventually pass, even though at the time, you may never feel like it is ever going to end.

Plus I would let Papa and my husband down if I gave up, I have too much to lose. But trust me, there are plenty of times where I have thought negative thoughts about myself and have doubted my ability. I mean, who am I to think I can achieve and succeed? What makes me so special, right? Let me tell you something, with an attitude like that, I would not succeed, and I would not have got anywhere in life! Even right now, as I write this book, I have only written 22,000 words! And already, I am thinking, how on earth am I going to achieve this? Am I actually going to write a book? I mean who actually cares, right!

These thoughts are common thoughts I am sure most of us think often throughout our day. But the trick is to NOT be consumed by these thoughts; change your thoughts! Writing a book is hard! But I am determined to get it finished, and do you know why? Well, for one reason, I have told some of my friends about writing a book, and this makes me accountable. And two, I really want to do this. I am determined to finish and succeed, because like I said, failing is not an option. I may come across obstacles along the way, like I have so far with not knowing what else to write, where will I start, am I writing enough? But I will just keep going.

Some days, I just wish I could sleep and not wake up. When I do wake up, I am glad though that I did actually wake up. I remind myself that giving up is not an option. You are on auto-pilot mode, you wake up, get up and get on with it—you keep going and never stop.

It's almost like you are in survival mode—according to Brene Brown, like being hijacked by the limbic system; this is called the emotional survival mode. There are periods that feel like darkest days. I learnt this saying from **Toni Christie**, owner of Childspace and a good friend of mine: "Fake it till you make it."

Some days, I did this really well, other days I thought, there is no way I can fake this! I then think of my brother-in-law and what I learnt from working for him—you can talk yourself into feeling great or not so great. If you think you are "good", you will be average and you will just be "good". However, if you think and say you are "fantastic" or "great" then you will become this and you will feel great. If you wake up in the morning and the frist thought you have is "I feel like shit, or today is going to be a shit day". What do you think is going to happen? Yep, you guessed it, you will have a shit day. So make the choice to wake up and say that everyday is going to be a great day, and watch what happens.

I chose to think and say to myself, "Sharon, you are doing the very best with what you can right now." But sometimes, saying it is the easy part—believing it is really hard. Life is not always going to go to plan, and you cannot control many things or even how other people act. The only thing you can control is yourself, your responses and how you act or react to situations.

As I was writing this in 2020, the world had been in a pandemic—Covid-19. New Zealand was in lockdown for four weeks in March. This year has been a really hard year for all of the world, but it has also had a positive impact on many, and I know for me, I have done a lot of personal growth and reflecting through this time. A lot of drinking and eating has also happened during this pandemic! And I remind myself every day—it's time to go for my run to lose all this weight! Tips on motivation and action may be another book, I think!

This same year I also went through a whole change in team, one after the other! I had hit rock bottom, again! I thought lots of negative thoughts. What is wrong with me? During this time, I began working on my personal and professional growth. I found a business coach, **Sarah Greener**, who helped me. Sarah was at times harsh and told me things I didn't want to hear, in that moment. But these were things that helped me. It is through this storm that I have really seen and felt that giving up is never an option.

I have learnt not to take things so personally and questioned whether I was responding positively to the change in my team. I was not prepared for this storm—yet interestingly, I had been through similar before, so why was this so different? My thoughts and my actions on how I was responding were what was different.

This storm took me by surprise and I was not prepared, and during the storm I had really negative thoughts and I was assigning blame instead of stopping and thinking that this is just a rocky storm that will pass so let's come up with a plan to get through it. I will talk more about looking at yourself in the mirror and asking, who is that person? What do you want to be known for and how are you showing up? But I learnt to look at myself and take responsibility for the hard times I have been through. I can't control how others are, but I can be responsible for the way I respond.

My husband owns his own business, and I also own my own business. People often think straight away, Oh, they must be rich! What people do not realise is that we have our whole life, our house, everything on the line for our businesses. If either of our businesses fail, we lose everything. Not wanting to put it negatively, but that is reality. And often I feel guilty for hiring someone to work for me for the day so I can get stuff done or just have some time. I work long hours at home, that no one sees and I too deserve time to rest. And yes, some may say I choose to have my own business, and yes, this is correct. I did and I still do want my business. Going through each storm is very scary, and sometimes I am not sure if I will get through the next one. When I look back after the storm has passed, things have worked out, but it's during the storm that I worry—as you just don't know how far away the next one is and how bad it may get. **Raewyn Weller** says, that if I am expecting another storm, I will get one. What we worry about, concentrate on, is what turns up in life.

Falling, Hurting and Getting Back Up

♥

"**Falling hurts, but getting back up helps you feel stronger.**"

At some point in all our lives, we are bound to fall. For instance, think about a young baby trying to roll over or walk. They fall or don't get it, but they keep trying and keep persevering until they master it. This is the same when we're teenagers or adults. Improving something you are not quite good at yet involves many failures along the way. For instance, Sir Edmond Hilary failed climbing mount Everest, but he didn't let that bother him—he kept going back until he succeeded. Mark Manson suggests that, "If someone is better than you at something, then it's likely because they have failed at it more than you have."

I've had my fair share of failures through my life. I know there will be plenty more to come. What I have learnt during times of falling down is that I am not best to be making decisions during the fall, it's like my brain gets all clouded. I may think I'm making the best decision, but I'm not—I'm acting out emotionally. Generally during a setback or fall, it can take me a few days to be able to clear my head and make decisions based on what I think may be the best decision at the time. We all feel and act out when we're emotional. I think, "I am such a failure." I shut down and feel really crappy. I don't want to hear what my husband wants to say, and I don't want him trying to fix it for me. Often, just having the time to myself to wallow and be inside my own head for a short while is what I need to begin with. I just want him to first of all listen to me and empathize with the situation.

When my head is clear and calm I'll then ask him to offer solutions, and it's here that I can be calm enough to stop, think, look in the mirror and ask myself, "How did I show up, and how did I respond to that situation? Could I have done anything differently?" Often when we fall or make mistakes, we're quick to blame other people—we couldn't possibly have played a part in any of it! And what this really is, is that we see blaming others as a quick fix. But owning our mistakes, reflecting and learning from our mistakes, while still loving ourselves, is one of the bravest and hardest things to do.

Don't get me wrong, we are not always to blame, but we do have a part to play in the blaming. For instance, if someone doesn't do a job for you the way you want it to be done, whose fault is that? At the time in your emotional state, you may get defensive and blame them. "Argh, but they didn't put the stapler back in the right place." And you'll say it's their fault. After calming down, you might then think, "Were you clear on where the stapler goes? Did they know where to put it? How are you responding to the situation?"

We are often so worried about what others will say or think about us, and this is human nature. However, I've come to realise that people are always going to judge and have their own opinions. Unfortunately, some don't keep their opinions to themselves. But these stories or judgements that other people may have about you are THEIR opinions. If you think about a time you've watched say the All Blacks, and say Dan Carter doesn't kick the ball over the post, we all sit in our chairs and say, "Oh, come on, Dan, I could have done that!" But could you have really? And do you think he's thinking, "Oh no, I can't play anymore! I'm so upset by what Sharon has said or thinks about me." He gets up and he learns from his mistakes. Hurt, suffering, failure, and disappointment happens to every single one of us. Another thing to have a think next time someone judges you or something you do. Think to yourself do they deserve to be in the arena with you (as Brene Brown would say). Unless they have walked in your shoes or experienced doing what you have, don't give their opinions a second thought.

Brene Brown says that vulnerability is the core of all emotions. She says that, "To feel is to be vulnerable." Oh, I so get this. Vulnerability is the foundation of the emotions and experiences that we crave. Being adaptable to change, having hard conversations, problem solving, being resilient, all takes vulnerability. There have been many times in my life I have felt vulnerable.

I remember when I was eighteen, and I separated from my daughter's father, this was one of the hardest things I have ever had to do. This was the first boyfriend I had to break up with. It wasn't long after this that I had a breakdown and isolated myself from everyone. I wasn't eating, and I looked terribly skinny. I wasn't looking after my two-year-old daughter properly because all I wanted to do was worry myself in self pity. I wasn't good enough. Of course I wasn't good enough. I said it to myself every day, and I started to believe it! My mum was constantly on my case about how skinny I looked and that I needed to go to counselling. I had hit rock bottom and didn't know how to get back up to the top. I had pushed away all my friends and my mum. I was not really heading anywhere, except to bed! This was one of my darkest times in my life. I was only eighteen, and I had no idea what was going on in my head, let alone in my life. My mum encouraged me to let my daughter go and live with her father for a while so could I work on myself. So we did this.

All I can remember from that time is getting out of the hole. I had to hit the bottom before I realised that I needed help and support. I was too stubborn to admit I needed support. I was too proud. But in the end, this is not good. I have learnt to take help when people offer help. I have learnt bottling the emotions up inside is not healthy or the right choice.

My advice if any of you are struggling: ask yourself: 'are you are too stubborn to accept help? Edmond Otis says "Resilient people ALWAYS ask for help". Allow yourself to go through it and feel the different emotions. Journalling can help with this. Get a pen and paper and just write. Write down what you thinking, how are you are feeling. What you think is happening? If you can't write, maybe you could draw? Maybe try meditating or going for a walk at a local park, sitting down and writing in a nice quiet space. How are you're feeling today, are you sad, angry or depressed, just know it is not how you'll always feel. Night time always turns into day and dark to light. Think of a time that you may have broken up with a partner—that feeling of rejection. For some, it takes months, even years to get over a breakup, but try to remember you can and will begin to feel happier again. Whatever your circumstances allow yourself the time to grieve or get over it. If you find yourself in a dark hole, with suicidal, or constant negative thoughts about harming yourself, please seek professional help. In NZ you can phone Lifeline: 0800 543 354, Youthline: 0800 376 633, or you can text them at 234. For agencies outside of NZ, you can google support and the numbers of your local area will come up. I have also added phone numbers at the reference of this book.

Try to remember a time when you were happy—what were you doing, where were you? Try to really imagine that feeling. Get in touch with friends or family, have talks with them about memories that make you laugh. Remember, when it rains, the sun will come back out—the sun will always shine again. When you go through struggles, there will be a light shining on the horizon. You'll get to that light, eventually. Just be kind and gentle to yourself—grieve, cry, scream. Allow yourself to feel all the emotions. And remember, you are not alone. There are people and professionals out there that care, if you need them.

A few months after Andrew and I broke up, I met my next partner, Richard, who helped slightly as I began to feel half human again. I began to have some better thoughts about myself.

We'd been together for a year when I got pregnant, and we had a baby together. Although he cheated on me while I was pregnant on a few occasions, when we had our daughter, he really stepped up and decided to make a go of our little family.

At this stage, I still didn't have my eldest daughter live with me, although I saw her every day. It wasn't until I began working at Tony's Tyre Service that I began to think positively and my mental attitude began to change. I grew apart from Richard, and after six and half years, we broke up.

And well, I then met my third baby's father, Stu. We married six years on, and almost eighteen years later, we're still together.

Looking back at what helped me over come one of my darkest times in my life, I cannot remember the exact remedy, and I think it would be different for each person. But one thing I do know is getting inside your head and all the negative thoughts is not healthy. We all do it, and later in my book I talk about the subconscious and conscious mind. Know that when we fall or make mistakes that the time will pass. We just have to give ourselves time and be kind to ourselves. Falling, no matter how many times, hurts. I hate to say it, but you will fall more than once or twice—in fact, if you want to get better at something you are bound to fall dozens of times—and I don't think you could say each fall will be easier or harder.

They will always hurt. Getting back up after a fall helps shape you into who you are. From the times I have fallen in my life, I know when I've gotten back up is when the learning really happens. Often when I have come across really hard times in my life, I've thought there are far more people out there in worse situations than me. There are people out there that don't have homes, food, or even family. I think we should count ourselves lucky and be grateful for every single day that we are alive.

Today I woke up, went to the gym and headed to work. I felt really positive and was excited to inform my team that I'd found the new teacher we'd been looking for. After ending the conversation, one of my teachers said to me she had a letter on my desk for me to read, and she said it was negotiable. My heart sank as I knew exactly what the letter was going to be. It was her resignation. ANOTHER resignation. I really don't think I can go through this again! I felt like I was going to vomit! Why me? Why is this happening again? I begin to question myself—what am I doing so wrong?

I went home to try to process this news, and yes, to allow myself to have a pity party. But I told myself, "You are only allowed to be in a pity party for today. Tomorrow, you must get up and face the world. Fake it till you make it! Yes, it's fuckin' hard at the moment, and guess what? Life is fuckin' hard." All these chapters without swearing—I'm not doing too bad yet! Raewyn Weller tells me that it will hard if I say so. Also people that swear are angry. I agree there was anger within me that I needed to let go.

I went to lunch with a friend and wallowed, then another great friend of ours phoned us, and I wallowed again. It wasn't till I said, "I love to challenge myself, but this challenge..." and then I stopped. We both laughed. This challenge is far too hard? I realised what I was saying, I mean, isn't any challenge hard? I really needed to listen to what I was saying—it's right now that I need to read my book and take the advice I've given! When things happen in our lives that we're not expecting, or we go through hard times, our mind goes into flight mode or emotional and survival centres of the brain. There is no way to make decisions when we're in this state of mind!

At the time, we think we're making the best decisions, or what we're thinking is great, but this is definitely NOT the time to be making decisions! Even right now as I write this, only a day has gone by, so I should still not be making any decisions, and trust me I'm not! I've had a chat with two of my great friends, and I'm currently drinking a bourbon. I'm still feeling self-pity and at times going into the whole, "but I could do better". What I need to realise is none of this is my fault. You see, I can't control what other people do, how they feel or their actions. I'm only in control of my response to this! So once I have finished my pity party, I'm going to come up with a plan. Now, don't think that it's okay to be in your pity party for too long. I say a day, but you don't want to be in this emotional brain any longer than that.

Sarah, my business coach, will say to me not to get into a pity party at all, but in reality, we all do it anyway, right? One thing I know for sure is there is no point in making decisions or a plan while you're in the emotional brain. These decisions will not be good ones. Managing a centre with staff is really challenging at times. Why me? What is so wrong with me, my centre? However, I can feel so rewarded at the same time! How is this even possible?

I started my business from nothing, and right after I graduated! This is such a big brave thing to do, and I actually would not recommend it to anyone! I learnt so much during my five and a half years in business with the centre. However with Stu also owning a business, my children growing up right before my eyes, and I was working over sixty hours each week, I made the hardest decision in my life to sell the centre. Not all those five and a half years were doom and gloom. Like I said, storms come and go, and you never know when the next storm is going to hit. Just like this storm - I was not fully prepared for it, and I'm not sure I will ever be fully prepared for all storms.

Everyone has a Story!

♥

"Never judge someone by their story"
When I began this journey of writing, I knew I wanted to share not only my story, but other people's stories too. I've always wanted to be a phycologist or look more into brain development. How other people respond to different situations, and the choices they make has always intrigued me. I also want you to know that you are not alone when going through hard times. You are not alone in your thoughts if you share them.

Most of us have been through some sort of trauma in our lives, but this does not have to define who we are. I am not saying you need to block out the trauma. Seek professional help from a trauma councillor if you need to. Talk about your experiences, but decide where you want to be with the experience. Do you want to be a victim, or do you want to be the survivor and inspire others? A traumatic experience doesn't have to rule or ruin your life.

I interviewed six people from different backgrounds, from young to old, well-off to not so well-off, and a foreign couple who came to NZ from South Africa in the '90s. I wanted to know how they defined resilience, what success meant to them and who or what influenced them. After, I will conclude if any of their outlooks are similar, or if they had anything in common.

Please also know that to protect them, I have used pseudonyms for them. The first person I will chat with is Bianca, who almost thirty years old—the youngest of my interviewees—then Judith, the oldest. Next will be Bill, an inspirational speaker, Pania, who grew up in poverty and finally Maria and Poes Kop, who moved to NZ from South Africa in 2001.

Bianca's Interview:

Bianca grew up with her mentally ill mum, who at times struggled with life. Because of this, Bianca spent many of her childhood years living with different family members. This never got her down or stopped her from wanting to achieve her goals. She has done really well for herself. I really admire Bianca, as she really understands her mum and is compassionate towards her—truly inspirational.

How do you define resilience?

No matter what you are faced with, you will constantly believe in yourself. Nothing is ever really too big that is going to get you down, you are always going to be on your own team. You build up that resilience. For me, I think I have had resiliency since I was a little girl. I have always imagined it as a concrete wall, that nothing can really take me down. You can stay confident and focus on yourself, and not care what anyone else thinks.

My most resilience would be my mum with her mental illness. It's daily resilience, since I was a child to now an adult. It's mentally taxing on myself, to know that it has nothing to do with me. Knowing that all the issues don't have anything to do with me, everyone is dealing with their own shit. So just focus on yourself.

What does success mean to you?

Funny, when I was younger I used to think it was money and possessions. I went travelling and worked in Australia, got the job and brought myself nice things. I then got a corporate job and thought, this is it! But I was still unhappy. And I realised that my happiest form was being at home with my partner, having less possessions to worry about and being self employed. Balancing social life and freedom.

Who is or has been your influence, if you have any?

My biggest influence would have to be my partner's family. I met my partner when I was 18, so his parents really taught me a lot through my teenage years. My partner was brought up with so much self-esteem. His parents have helped us with business, guiding us with money, etc. I believe in myself, they have been a huge impact on my life. When I was younger, I always had resilience and believed in myself, having my partners family has just added another layer.

Another role model would be my Aunty B. I used to go there every school holidays, she's very driven and creative. She has her own style, she is very similar to me. I was always super influenced by what she did.

Judith's Interview:

Judith suffered from depression on a different level than most of us would ever imagine. What I admire about Judith, and one of the reasons why I chose her to interview, is how she managed to stay happily married to her husband for 60 years and raised four beautiful girls, who have all grown up now and have children of their own. Family is important to them, and this is an inspiration to me!

How do you define resilience?

The earliest memories I have is when I was about two-ish. We lived with this old man, we were looking after him. I remember I used to go in and see him every morning, and tell him breakfast was ready. One morning, I went in and he was on the floor, he went to hospital, and I think he must have died because we then had to move.

When I was ten we moved into a house with my uncle who was not a very nice man, so at fifteen or sixteen I moved to Palmerston North and boarded with an aunty and uncle. I then moved back to Wellington, which is where I met Brian, and at twenty we married, then at twenty one we had our first daughter, then four daughters later.

Unfortunately, after having my third daughter I suffered from a bad break down. I think I suffered from depression as a child actually. So anyway, they send me down to Porirua hospital—which was a dreadful place. I had about five lots of shock treatment. Eventually, I signed myself out. The doctor said, "You are not ready to go, I guarantee you will be back." I was told I wasn't allowed to have any more children. At thirty, I got pregnant again, I had the baby. There was a huge hooha.

Most of my life I have been up and down, but I suppose I am resilient. You can't explain why this happens. We had nothing and tried to buy a business with nothing. My husband has now passed away, I miss him terribly. My resiliency is this kind of thing.

I often wonder what have I achieved, the first thing I think about is my four children. Pulling myself out of the hole was not easy. When I had the break down, I didn't know what was happening to me, I thought I must be going mad. Depression is a real thing, in those days it wasn't talked about much. But it's so important to talk about it, to not be ashamed. But all in all, I went through that—and I survived! Often, when things like this happens marriages break up.

I did a lot of evening work to give us a bit more income. It was hard, it really was.

In my opinion, this lady is a inspiration. Judith has done an amazing job of raising four girls, who have all turned out great, with children of their own. She is so humble.

Who is or has been your influence, if you have any?

Brian was very influential. I can see more things about him now that he is gone. I am very determined and want things done now. He was the calm one, who always said "just take it easy". He still influences me today. I think about what we would he do – whenever I am not sure what to do.

Judith met her husband at eighteen years old, they had been together for sixty years. I think this is a success!

There's definitely ups and downs—it wasn't always plain sailing.

Bill's Interview:

Bill is a successful businessman, well known in New Zealand. He is also an inspirational speaker. I chose Bill because he has inspired me, and I know he is also a human just like you and I. He had a vision, he knew what he wanted and what he didn't want in life. He achieved some goals, and he also failed at times, but he never gave up.

How do you define resilience?

No matter what the challenges are, being able to work through them, don't give up till you find a solution. And if you can't find a solution, you have to accept that it is what it is really and just move on to the next thing.

Every step along the way, challenges are thrown at everyone in life, it's how we deal with them. I think of a saying, "If you've got control of it, you shouldn't worry about it". That's all well in practice, people always worry about things they have no control over. Everyone has doubt within themselves and their abilities.

One situation with a house I wanted to buy, I had been promised some funding for this house. We put an unconditional offer on this house before selling our existing house. Then the day before, the bank phoned and said we can't do this. So I thought, "What do I do hear?" My only solution was to go to Auckland, I sat down outside the CEO of Westpac's office until he answered my call. Resiliency "never say die until it comes to the end, and sometimes it does."

What does success mean to you?

Lots of people say all these fluffy things, anyone can say those things really. But in reality success is achieving something that you never thought you would achieve, it's achieving beyond what you ever accepted. Bringing other people along the way to enjoy some of that success, or create a situation so they can be successful too. It gives you a great deal of satisfaction. And then of course there's being a good father, the best you can, we all fail in times. I never failed a thousand times, I just learnt how to not do it a thousand times.

Who is or has been your influence, if you have any?

Life is the influence, there was not really one person who has influenced me in a negative or positive way. I knew what and what I didn't want. I knew I wanted to buy my own home, as growing up we always lived in rented homes, so I knew I didn't want to do that. It was the situations that were and are the influence.

Poes Kop & Maria's Interview:

Poes Kop and Maria are great friends of Stu and me. We met years ago at the squash club. They are South African, and came to NZ in 2001 with their two young children, leaving all of their family behind in South Africa!

Over the years, we have had many get togethers and each time they share a new story about their life back in South Africa. Their stories have always amazed me, and I can never quite comprehend the life they lived, the strength they show and the resilience to not give up on each other.

I do not doubt they have had many close calls regarding ending their relationship—as many of us have—I think we would be lying if we said our relationships have always been stable with no arguing, but for all the life experiences they have had, and their life in NZ with no family, this to me is an inspiration.

Interviewing Poes Kop and Maria brought up many emotions and stories for them as I sat and listened. I also reflected on how you never really know what other people have been or are going through. You might meet someone who lives a great, happy life, with a nice home and great relationship. But their life most likely wasn't always like that. Everyone starts somewhere, or may have had nothing. In order to achieve something, you will start from the bottom, whatever the bottom may look like for you.

Poes Kop and Maria wanted a better life and future for their children and grandchildren, but in order to do this they had to sacrifice by leaving their family and friends behind in South Africa to move to New Zealand. They story is very touching and inspirational. I told them both this interview would only take fifteen minutes—THREE hours later and us all in tears, I have a great story to share with you.

We decided we were going to make it, nothing was going stop us, and not look back. When we moved to NZ, some days we cried our eyes out—it was so hard. Because it was just us, you just bit the bullet. But that was the hardest part for us, and that's the resilience.

I find it so empowering that you came here. You didn't know anyone, you left all your family behind. If you got into an argument with each other, you would have nowhere to go.

No, we didn't argue, we were very strong. It was very hard. We had to be strong for each other and the children. When we got here, we didn't look for South Africans. It took us a very long time to settle in.

I remember when I got a job and the kids had to bike to school, they were about nine and eleven. We were so stressed the kids had to bike over two streets, in South Africa they would get dropped off to the day care lady, who would then walk them to school.

I grew up rich but poor, my dad worked sixteen hours a day. Maria grew up poor. All Maria's wages were given to her mum, at least half of her salary. Maria never had help with her English at home as her mum could not speak English. So her mum couldn't help her with her homework, so the kids just help each other as much as they can. My dad lost his arm working as a shunter on the railways, in a work accident. He worked sixteen hours a day, seven days a week. I thought, I am not going to be like my dad, I am not going to work that hard.

When we came to NZ, we came over with the points system, it took us a year to get all the paperwork together to get here. It was certainly not easy. We told our family we were moving—they were like, "WHAT?" Maria's family were okay, my family was a tight-knit family. They were against us every time we phoned, they said, "Why don't you come back?" We would see photos of them partying together. That was really tough. We used to have themed parties all the time. We had babies together. But we were really tough, when one of us was down, the other would lift the other up.

Poes Kop came over for four and a half months before Maria, and he got really down without his family.

How do you define resilience?

You put your mind to something and go through with it, you have a goal. Everything we did wasn't easy, but we had to make it, you take the negatives and run with the positives. At the end there is not a lot of things that stop you. Learn through the process, with the goal we had to come here, nothing was going to stop us. Sports-wise, when I was young I achieved a lot, sport was my drive. Maria adds Poes Kop achieved everything he could to the highest, he worked really hard, and sometimes he got to the top. School-wise, Poes Kop didn't really care about school. Sport-wise he hated losing, so that was his drive. He was very competitive and practised till he got to the top, or he could beat them.

I don't want to lose, because you don't want to lose, the negatives come. And you keep trying till you win. Poes Kop justifies why he didn't like losing.

Poes Kop talks about the first two years of living in NZ was really hard, but they stuck at it. Their first Christmas, they had been here for three month, Poes Kop decided he would dress as Santa—he put a note in the neighbours letterboxes. As they tell the story, we begin to cry, so we are all sitting around with tissues. It was hard, we toughed it out though.

He said, *If you want to be there, bring a gift for Santa. The morning of we could not believe it – there were so many people, everyone came! They brought platters, some food we had never had before. The bell rang, about 9:00am in the morning, dropping off presents for the children. At 10:00am when it started there were kids and parents everywhere. We didn't know them at all! That's how we made friends. It was so special. In the evening, we phoned our family back in South Africa. We went through so many emotions. We would be happy then, and then we would cry. This is how we showed resilience. We just carried on through.*

Poes Kop started getting out, playing cricket and darts. Maria was staying at home, watching the kids.

We knew we could have found the South African groups, but we wanted to learn the Kiwi way first. So we had to tough it out. This made us tough and closer as a family. Our son struggled a bit, so we got him into squash, we did this as a family.

Poes Kop says Maria was tougher than he was, her family had travelled, they did a lot on their own and had moved. He hadn't moved. Poes Kop says he can achieve and be whatever he would like to be.

But I don't think we will ever move again. If we have to we will. But we are settled, we would not go through that again.

Being around positive people. We had no family here, so we could not lose our jobs. We had no one to turn to. No brothers to stay with. But we knew we would survive. We just had each other to rely on.

What does success mean to you?

Marriage is a huge success—we have been together for so many years. Maria was the glue, she kept us together.

Success is where you put your goals. If I put my goals and I reach them I then feel fulfilled. Squash was one of them, I got to C1, and then once I got there I went further and aimed higher. I felt great when I achieved something.

Maria said for her it's her running.

Once I achieved the 10k, I have succeeded. Passing my courses through work is success. The success of coming over here, wow, that was a huge success, getting the papers, there were certain jobs we had to do to come over here on the point system.

Poes Kop continues.

Success to me is, when we could buy our first house. We had nothing when we got together. Buying our first home was massive. Every time we have achieved everything we wanted to achieve we felt successful. We had no money, we had to work hard for everything we had. We had no help from anyone. Moving into our own home, we felt great, we actually felt like grownups!

I put a goal, and I work hard for what I get, and this is success. I feel so good for this. Success is all the little goals we have achieved, success was when my daughter walked in and got married, our kids will be good and happy. We want to see our kids happy. We don't have ten houses. Some people say that having ten houses is success. We made it in NZ and that is success. Our kids have good jobs, their success is our success. We have to work hard for what we have. Nothing has been handed to us. Success to us is all the little things, when my daughter walked in and got married. She has got a good husband, so we can take responsibility for raising our children. We made it in NZ, that to us is success. We look back and say to each other, we did it, man, we did well!

Who or what has influenced you? Or influences you now?

Poes Kop says his dad was his influencer—just with his morals.

His whole life was so driven for what he wanted to achieve, and he had nothing! He was just a very hard worker. My dad had one arm, he was driven and dedicated. He got us out of poverty, he helped me with the first bike I wanted to buy. This influenced me to want to be a dad to my children like him. We had no TV, I will never forget how determined my dad was. There was a boxing match on, we went to a place like Harvey Norman, called Russells. They had all the TVs in the windows. Inside, there were people inside watching and drinking. My Dad and I were on the pavement, watching the boxing from there.

As we walked away, Dad said, "Stuff it, we are going to buy a TV, I am not this low." The next day he brought a TV. So I went to school the next day and told my friends, "We have a TV." My dad worked so hard. A TV till this point was not a priority. Everything in our house was paid for, he would not buy anything if he didn't have the money. His house was paid off as soon as he could. He would save and save. He worked sixteen hours a day.

Maria says Poes Kop is her influencer.

He drives me to be the best I can. And out of my family, I think it would be my mum would have influenced me.

Pania's Interview:

Pania was my lecturer, we became really great friends. Pania has taught me so much about myself and what I can achieve. Pania grew up in poverty, in a world some of us can never imagine. Everyone has a story—we are all humans who feel the same emotions, our hearts beat and our blood flows the same in everyone.

How do you define resiliency?

Resiliency is not giving up, it is proving people wrong, and I would probably say that resiliency for me would be being able to persevere with challenges that come up against me in life. Other people may see this as an obstacle, however I see this as a positive as these situations teach me something.

Has this helped you at different times in your life?

When I was younger, I didn't grow up in a very supportive home, I was not supported by my siblings, I was always told I was dumb—stupid. I don't remember my mum helping me often, she was a single mum raising five children. I was the middle child of the five. No one was there to read my books when I came home from school, so I would just read to myself.

I didn't have anyone driving me, and I also didn't have anyone telling me I was good enough either. So I believe that in turn this has driven me to succeed at stuff. It was never encouraged in the home to further our education. I want my children to see me succeed. And actually, my daughter does tell me I have been a great role model to her. My daughter has seen how much I have struggled and succeeded.

What does success mean to you?

Success is happiness on the inside, being happy with myself, what I have achieved. Which I don't think I am quite there yet. I know that there is more that I want to succeed in. One of my biggest goals is to own my own house. I want something to leave behind for my children. So success for me is actually success for my children. When I am old, my children are looking after me.

Who or what has influenced you? Or influences you now?

In the past, other people, like my older sisters, they both had the same drive as me. Especially my older sister, she was the first one in our family to get a degree. So when she achieved that, I thought, "I can do that too."

Other people that have influenced me are strong people, being able to navigate their life the way they want to. Even though they have been judged or people say things about them, they have had an impact on me. At a job I worked at a few years ago, there was a Maori woman who worked with me. She encouraged me, pushed me to do things out of my comfort zone.

Conclusion of the Interviews:

Isn't it interesting how different we all are? We all have different drives, wants and desires. This, I believe, is why we are all unique. We all have stories to be told, but in the end we can all be successful and influenced by those around us or life in general. Each of the five people I interview all experienced times in their lives where they were resilient. They fought through and succeeded. Have a think about your life. What does success mean to you? And who influences you? Are you where you want to be in your life right now? If you aren't, what do you need in order to get there? All the interviewees worked hard for the things they wanted to achieve—and in some cases they had to work harder—but they never gave up.

Thank you again to those who gave me their time and for letting me share your stories about getting through difficult times.

Tools that helped me

♥

"*Finding ways that help live the best life*"

I am going to give you some information about different tools that have helped me at different times in my life. Every situation or struggle that we face in life is often presented differently each time, and what works one time may not necessarily work another time you struggle. This is something that I've experienced and found. Not all of these tools worked in the order that they are written. I hope you find something from this that works for you, but if you don't, that is okay. I suggest you keep trying to find solutions that do fit. Keep reading, talking and looking for the answers.

We all go through difficult times in our lives, and some are definitely worse than others, but how we respond to these struggles and difficult times can either help us or break us. Some of us always need to be the victim and may try all different ways, but until we work within ourselves and look at how we are showing up, how we are responding and changing our mindset to more positive thoughts, our lives may not change. We are the thoughts that we think, and the way we act or feel is how we create our lives.

I think sometimes, when we go through something or we just feel something—like depression—we don't even know what we're feeling, or why we're feeling the way we're feeling. For me, when I went through my break down at the age of eighteen, I don't remember what it was exactly that helped me get through. It was just time, and probably having a strong mindset of determination. I remember when people would ask me how I was or want to help, I would push them away or ignore them. I didn't want to deal with the issues at that time. It's almost like something just clicked in me, I had to hit the very bottom in order to begin the journey back to the top. And I had to be ready to ask for the help I needed in order to get back to the top. But you don't need to wait till you hit rock bottom to ask for help, I would not recommend this at all. It's important to accept help, ask for help. Talk to someone, anyone that you trust. Reach out. When things begin to feel overwhelming, make sure you let someone know how you are feeling. There is always a solution, and in some cases there are people who have been through what you're feeling, so they may know how to help. Or you might just need someone to listen to you.

Today when I go through hard times or I begin to feel down, I am older—and some may say, wiser—so I can deal with things differently. Working on yourself, letting go of the past, accepting what is—it takes a long time. Any form of healing does not take over night, and you do need to put in the energy to work on it. So please do not expect changes or to feel complete over night.

Now in my life, instead of shutting down and shutting out those in my life who care, I let them know I just need a bit of space, or I go for a walk or a run. I still get those negative thoughts in my head, "Oh Sharon, you are fat. You need to do this or that," but I very quickly remove these negative thoughts and replace them with positive thoughts, "You are a beautiful person, there is no one like you." Replacing your negative thoughts with positive thoughts takes time, so be gentle and kind to yourself! And most of all—do the work!

Below, I would like to share with you seven of the tools that have helped me at different times when I've struggled. I hope you find one or more of these tools helps you. What I would suggest is to find what resonates with you. Keep going back and reading those tools as often as you need. Keep a diary of what is and isn't working.

Wellbeing

Looking after yourself would have to be the number one thing that I think you should do! I'm starting this chapter off with a monthly challenge for you. I will go more into these challenges throughout the tools and refer back to this challenge.

My challenge to you is to get a yearly planner or diary. Take a look at my website, you can download or purchase a printed copy of a journal I've designed. Each month, set yourself a challenge for that month. I have listed some ideas here. If something hasn't quite worked or it has, share your story with me! Send me an email, I would love to hear from you! Tell me how your challenge has or hasn't worked.

Look after yourself, Listen to your body. If you're tired, rest, sleep. If you're hungry, eat. If you need to cry, cry. It's so easy to give this advice to others! I haven't always looked after myself and my wellbeing, often putting myself last—not intentionally, its just happened that way.

Do you ever find yourself giving your friends advice about how they should look after themselves or listen to their body? I find it super easy to give this advice, but when it comes to me, I must admit I have not always been the greatest at taking this advice!

When I owned my childcare centre, there were days I had to work very long hours as we were short staffed. At times I went without a lunch break. I always put my staff before myself, and if it meant missing out, that was okay. I would never do this on a long term basis as this is not sustainable, but as a leader, sometimes you do need to come last. For me, my wellbeing was running, going to the gym, having a bourbon at the end of the day while I would cook dinner—Hmm, okay, maybe a couple! We all have different ideas about what looking after our wellbeing looks like, and no one is right or wrong. I think as long as you are aware of listening to your body and looking after it by taking time out when you need to, you are doing great. I mean, in all honestly, how can you look after others, or even be there for others, if you can't look after yourself? Since I've begun this journey of writing this book, I have had many ups and downs and have certainly learnt the importance of my wellbeing. My body lets me know pretty quick if there is something wrong and I'm not listening to it.

A conference I went to in Australia, hosted by early childhood consultants Semann & Slattery, reminded me of hope and gratitude, so each day I write down what I'm grateful for. I also message close friends to tell them that I am grateful for them and the things they do for me. It's really helped me change my negative thoughts by focusing on positive, kind thoughts. It's interesting that we all generally remember our negative memories and dwell on these before we remember our positive memories. Let the negative memories go! In order to begin feeling good—you first need to stop feeling bad!

Previously, I suggested you challenge yourself with being **grateful each day.** I suggest you buy any journal or book you can write in. Be thankful for eleven things every day, and call up your friends and tell them you appreciate them. Being grateful really helps you appreciate what you have in life. **Surround yourself with the people** and the things that bring you pleasure.

Immerse yourself in nature at least once a week. In some of the times, when I was in those dark places, I would go for a walk or spend time at the beach. This is always really therapeutic for the soul. I would sit on the beach with a diary and just write down my thoughts, or what I was grateful for. Getting out in nature, walking or exercising is known and believed to be good for mental health. Some people enjoy yoga or meditation. I really enjoy running. I find running helps me – it clears my mind. I put my ear plugs in and just let myself wander where - ever my mind takes me. I used to listen to music when I ran, but recently I have begun listening to positive self-help audio books.

After having my youngest daughter, I had kidney disease. The doctors decided to take the kidney out as it was only functioning at 8% efficiency, and it was causing more grief than anything. When the doctor told me this, I thought I was going to the appointment to be discharged from the hospital, so to be told this news was a shock! I remember crying on the lift and phoning Stu, telling him they were going to operate and take my kidney! Your wellbeing and taking care of yourself is super important—one day you have all your organs but the next day you may not! This is where I suggest living your life in balance. I have never been one to watch what I eat—I don't eat badly, I just don't eat an amazing diet—but now with only one kidney, I really do need to look after the one I have. There is no way I want to lose that one! So being careful about what I eat and drink and the medications I can and can't take is important to me. It's amazing how different you feel when you **eat wholesome food** rather then sugary, fatty food. **Challenge yourself in your yearly planner**. For a month, write down what you eat, how you feel, and how you sleep!

A couple of years later, I still had the pain, and when I was thirty I had to have a hysterectomy as I had endometriosis. Although, it took years and years of me fighting for them to diagnose this! If anyone reading this has had endo you will know the pain and the suffering us women go through and the years of years of fighting to get a diagnosis! Going through something like this can really get you down and depressed. You have to take time off work, and your young children watch you in so much pain that you can't walk.

There are days when I really don't want to exercise, but I know that once I get out there I will feel good. I've heard a saying that action comes before motivation, and I find if I think about things too much, I can talk myself out of going. So I just say to myself, "Sharon, you need to go for a walk or a run—you know you enjoy it." I always enjoy the feeling after going for a walk or run – its the feeling of making myself go that is hard.

I also consider spending time with my husband, daughter and friends to be part of my wellbeing. Since I started my business five years ago, I find that I don't have as much time for my husband. I go to bed earlier, I get up earlier, and I often bring work home as well! I am getting better at this lately, but before lockdown, I was really bad and constantly worked! For some people this is okay, but I needed to spend time with my family and friends. Laughter and socialising with great friends is good for the soul. I remember I was really down on myself some nights. We had a dinner on or something, and I wouldn't want to go, but when I got there I would cheer up really fast as I know being around my friends is always great for laugh. One other suggestion I have is, if you don't already, do what lights you up! Set time aside for yourself at least once a week—whether it's to paint, bake, take photos. Be creative, listen to your favourite music, take up a new hobby—maybe something you've been wanting to for a long time. Do more of what makes you happy and smile!

Limit your time on social media. It can be a negative and not good for our wellbeing. Let's face it, we—well mostly women—tend to compare ourselves to others. We watch Jill, a Facebook friend, posts all the amazing things she's doing. She is looking so great! She is always away, doing fun things. We wish we had her life or looked as good as she does at twenty-five.

Let me tell you, this is not healthy. Facebook is not real! People only post positive, amazing photos of themselves! Unless you can 100% say you don't ever compare yourself to others or think like that about who is on your page, Facebook, any social media can screw up your mind.

I was one of these people, but who were my friends on Facebook? What were they offering positively for me? I went through my friends list and deleted a few friends that I really didn't need, or I didn't see in real life! This was extremely hard for me! I went through my Facebook friends one by one and thought, "Do you add value to me, are we actually friends?" If the answer was no or I wasn't too sure, I deleted them. Before I knew it, I'd deleted a few people who I thought I didn't need on my page.

I know we all take Facebook so personally. If someone deletes us, we think, "Oh, my god! *What have I done? Why has my old high school friend deleted me? We don't ever talk or comment on Facebook, but they deleted me!*" We take it personally! Deleting these people off my Facebook does not mean I do not like them or would not say "hi" to them at the supermarket. I just do not need to have everyone that I don't really have a friendship with on my Facebook. If I think about the people who are influencing me, social media is one of the strongest, and I currently only want to be inspired and influenced by positive minded people.

I challenge you to go through your Facebook friends too. Do you have four hundred friends? Or more? How many of them would you buy dinner if you were to go out? How many of your Facebook friends would you stop and talk to if you saw them at the local grocery store? And who would you avoid? I challenge you to go through and delete the friends on Facebook that don't add value to your life or who you wouldn't stop and talk to at the grocery store. If you do this exercise and delete any of your face book friends, message me and let me know how it went. How do you feel, what are your thoughts? I would love to know!

Sleep well, take a bath or shower before you go to bed each night. Stay off technology at least half an hour before you go to bed, and turn TV off at the same time.

Listen to nice, calming, relaxing music. Music is medicine. Put lavender on your pillow. Ensure you get the sleep you need each night—the amount varies for each of us. I love my sleep, so this is easy for me to do! But I know when I am stressed or have something on my mind, I struggle to get to sleep. Listening to calming music or mindfulness apps that you can download on your phone, sometimes helps.

So it's super important to look after yourself. **Listen to your body and your intuition**, and keep going back to the doctor if something does not sit! I met a lovely lady Raewyn in Whakatane when I was on holiday. She wrote a book titled, "Your Health is Your Greatest Wealth". She talks about how we can all heal each cell in our body through reprogramming your mind, every cell—just not our teeth. Great book to read if you want to go more into healing your body. I will add details at the end of this book for you to reference.

Instruction Manual for Life

♥

This chapter is an instruction manual for life, that was gifted to me by Raewyn Weller. I hope you find this helpful, and thank you Raewyn for allowing me to add this to my book.

We are born without an instruction manual, we learn everything we know about the world and ourselves along the way from parents, peers, siblings, partners, teachers etc, be it positive or negative. We collect experiences that shape us in every moment of our exsitence: anxious or very social, cheerful or grumpy, tolerant or impatient.

Some people focus mainly on their jobs and careers, some on their familes, some don't care about anything but themselves. Some of us are good and some of us have a harder time handling the situations that life throws at us.

But in each of us, there is something that can always be improved and changed.

How would you feel if you were a little more patient or maybe more organized?

Is it possible to overcome your boredom and start being more productive instead of procrastinating all the time?

Or think about the owerwhelming moments of anxiety and stree. Do you wish you could know how to get through them more easily?

We often face situations where we cannot control something, which of course can be frustrating. We are beings who want to contol rahter than be controlled. But what most of us do not realise – is that the most important thing is to be able to control ourselves, our thoughts and our emotions.

Remember, the words we say and the pictures we create in our mind, Creates our life.

Imagine what it would be like to have an instruction manual for your mind!

We each see and interpret things differently based on past experiences and programming. Our representation of the world largely determines what our experience of the world is, how we perpecive the world, what options we see available to us as we live and how we react to every circumstance we encounter.

We already have all the resources we need.

No one is wrong. Humans function perfectly to achieve what they currently achieve.

Everything just is.

There is no such thing as failure, there is only feedback, lessons to learn.

Communication is more than what you say.

If you don't get the answer you want, try something different.

Each behaviour is useful in a specific context.

Behind every behaviour is a positive intention.

We all have choices, having a choice to make is better than no choice at all.

TAKE CONTROL OF YOUR LIFE TO AVOID TURNMOIL AND EXPERIENCE LOVE AND PEACE.

Having and Setting Goals

♥

"People with goals most likely succeed because they know where they're going."

Having goals, small or big goals, something to look forward to or work towards, can help when you are stuck and aren't sure where you're heading, or if you are feeling overwhelmed with life in general. Something as small as getting out of bed every day is a goal for someone—especially when you're feeling so low that you don't want to get out of bed. Getting out of bed means you have to face the world, right? How often have you stuffed up or done something you were not proud of? Facing the world or anyone is the hardest thing to do! Well, put it this way, you have no option! You have to get up and you have to face those people!

Trust me, at the time you won't want to, and you will feel sick, but once you've faced what you needed to, it will make it easier to do it again. Staying in bed and running away from your problems is not really an option. Decide what matters the most to you—let go of the things you can't control or don't really want. Surround yourself with the things that bring you pleasure. Let go of the things you don't want, no longer need, or the things that are not serving you and have a negative impact on you. Write a list if you need to, and then work on the first thing on the list that you know you can achieve! If you have a yearly planner, write in your thoughts and achievements each day.

Goal setting can be really hard for some, if not most of us—and for some of you goal setting will be new. You may not know where to start to achieve your goal, or to even come up with a goal!

My suggestion is, if everything is feeling overwhelming for you, you have goals but you are just not achieving them. Or you don't know what to make your goal. Write in your journal or yearly planner. Begin writing all the things you want in life, no matter how big or small. Write it all down. Even if you're sure you won't achieve the goal—I still want you to write it down. To begin with, I suggest starting with three goals. It might go something like this:

1. Buy my first house. By 2025 I am going to save $100 each week in order to be able to buy my first house.

2. Walk the dogs everyday. For eight weeks, I am going to get up every morning and take the dogs for a walk around the block before doing my morning routine.

3. Finish writing my book. By March 2023 I will dedicate one hour each week to writing in my book in order to have it finished by March.

These are great goals, but you might be thinking, *"How on earth are we going to achieve them?"* Goals setting can be overwhelming and scary!

My first piece of advice is, write down your goal. What do you want to be, do, or have? If you think, *"What's the point? I will not achieve this goal,"* I still want you to write it down, no big or small, and no matter how silly the goal feels!

As you write your goal down, think about it being specific and time-bound—set a time you will achieve the goal by. Be realistic. If you want to take the dogs for a walk every day, but you really know you won't have the time to do that, start off with the goal of taking the dogs for a walk three times a week for six weeks, then increase it. Sometimes, breaking the goal right down really helps, and once you see that you're achieving it, you want to keep going and reach more goals! Start with small goals that you know you can and will achieve! If your goal is too big and takes too long for you to achieve, you will quickly lose focus and give up working on it.

If you need to, go back to my chapter on Determination where I explain setting goals using the SMART goal method.

After you have written your goal out, carry it around with you, or hang it on your fridge or computer. Look at it on a daily basis. If you find yourself reverting back to those negative thoughts like, *"What am I thinking? I will never achieve this goal. That goal is far too out of my reach,"* read the goal you have written, remember the feeling you had when you first wrote the goal down and imagine yourself having achieved the goal. Really feel what it feels like to have accomplished it. Imagine that feeling of satisfaction and how proud you will be of yourself. You need to visualise and really imagine yourself achieving your goal. A great book to read is "Into the Magic Shop" from James R Doty. I highly recommend this book if you are struggling with believing in yourself or seeing yourself achieving your goal. I have referenced the book at the end.

Revisiting your goals can be important too as sometimes we make our goals far too big, not really achievable, or a goal that is likely to take us ten years to achieve! I mean, in all honesty, if I set myself a goal that I wanted to achieve in ten years, I would likely lose interest. I would need to break the goal right down into steps I could take to get to the goal. Somehow make yourself accountable—tell someone you trust about your goal and get them to check in with you to help you keep on track.

It is said that people who write down their goals and read them on a regular basis are more likely to achieve them. For me, this has certainly been the case. The more I've read my goal or envisioned it, the more I was determined and likely to achieve it! Let's say you are feeling lousy and don't want to face your life, your goal might be getting yourself out of bed. We need to be specific about the goal and make it achievable, and we also want it to be inspiring. So it might go something like, *"This week, I will get out of bed four days out of seven so I can spend time with my dogs."* Great! So now you will visualise yourself getting out of bed and walking the dogs. And what incentive will you have when you get out of bed? What will the consequence be if you don't get out of bed, other thena the dogs hanging around with a sad dace wanting a walk? You need to make yourself accountable, so phone a close friend, your partner, Mum or Dad and tell them your goal, your incentive, and the consequence. You want your goal to be achievable so you get that amazing feeling when you achieve the goal! It really is like an adrenalin rush! If you remember reading about my friend Pops Koe, he was very competitive when it came to sports. He always wanted to do better and beat the other person. This was his goal, and he was determined and kept trying and going until he achieved it.

In the past, I know when I've achieved my goals I've felt so damn excited. I've wanted to yell out to the world about the excitement I felt. This feeling is so amazing that once you achieve that small goal, your next goal can be slightly more challenging—possibly to get out of bed seven days out of seven! You can reach your goals! You just need to believe it and then act on it! I also remember the challenge, and how hard I've had to work at achieving my goals! Just like now, while I write the rest of my book. I have 5,000 words left to write, my goal was to write 60000 words —I am so close, but yet it's sooo hard! I just keep reminding myself about the prize at the end of it—the feeling of getting to the finish line and achieving! This is what is keeping me going. And also, I've told a few people about writing a book—so I kind of have to finish it!

A few years ago my best friend lost her brother to suicide. I remember thinking how was I going to help take the pain away, and in all fairness, I actually couldn't have taken that pain away. I didn't have any answers, and the only thing I could think of was to be there for her, show her support and let her know I was there any time she needed me. After a few months, I could still see the pain in her eyes, so I suggested to her that she and I go to Sydney to see her sister and the Gold Coast for our thirtieth birthdays. So we made a plan and set ourselves a goal. Although this did not take away the pain, and I'm not sure anything ever takes away the pain of losing someone, this gave my friend something to look forward to, and I know her seeing her sister would have meant a lot to her.

Making this goal for the both of us was exciting. We motivated each other and kept eachother accountable. We all love that feeling of having something to look forward to. And an even better feeling is when the day arrives when we've accomplished our goals. But watch out! Achieving your goals can be addictive. Once you achieve the first goal, you will most definitely want to move on to the next goal. And in life, sometimes you can't reach all of your goals, or you have to work extra hard to achieve them. At times it feels like you will never get there! I guess this all depends on how badly you really want something and the lengths you will take to achieve your goals. I'm sure determination and resilience often plays a huge part in achieving some goals. But believe in yourself! You can achieve anything you set your mind to! Now is the time for ACTION!

Read, read and read, or listen to podcasts or audible books

During the Covid-19 lockdown, I found myself listening to many inspiring podcasts while I went for runs. A friend of mine mentioned that she listens to books on Audible. I really thought I could not do that, but then I thought I would give it a go, and wow, I really enjoyed it! I read a book first and then listened to the same book on Audible—crazy, you may think. But, I actually got different things out of the book after listening to it on Audible! As a young child, I used to read a lot. I remember taking books with me and reading wherever we went. But as I grew older, I stopped reading, and became so busy. Taking up reading again, I got addicted to it. I read self-help books, books about intuition and spiritually, every book that interested me and of course helped me at the same time. At the end of this book I'll write a page dedicated to books I recommend you read. Sometimes, even reading other peoples stories is helpful when you are going through struggles. This helps you know you are not the only one ever going through struggles, and trust me—there are always worse off people out there then ourselves!

Reading can add so much value to your life! Not to mention educate you. If it's a fiction book you enjoy reading, it's still adding positive value to your life.

At the beginning of this book you may remember I mentioned the twelve monthly challenge for the yearly planner? One of the challenges was to read or listen to podcasts. Gaining new knowledge and learning helps the brain and making connections. This helps with so many things, such as memory—not to mention, gaining knowledge that we can then share with our family and friends!

If you have small children and find it hard to read because you just don't have the time, I would highly recommend Audible—you can put your ear plugs in while the kids are watching TV, or even when they've gone to bed! Jump into bed, or even run yourself a nice bath, and either read a book or listen to a book on Audible. If you are not interested in reading, YouTube, Ted Talks or podcasts are great to watch online. There are so many inspiring people out there talking online all the time, so take the time each week to listen to them. Google what interests you. Google is my best friend!

Believing in yourself

Although this is at times really hard to do, you should believe in yourselves. There is only ever one of you! You are special, you are unique, there is NO ONE that will ever be like you! I found this very hard to do as a teenager.

Because we moved around a lot, I struggled with how to fit in. I remember having a nice group of friends in my first year of high school. Then, I don't know what happened, but the next thing I knew, they were bullying me! One day, walking home from school, three of the girls followed me and threatened to give me a hiding. You'd think with all the violence I'd seen that I should be able to stick up for myself, but I clammed up. I knew the guy at the dairy quite well, so I ran in there and hid behind the counter for safety. I was so scared! Eventually, they left. I went home and told my mum. She phoned the police and the school. There was no way I was going back to that school! This affected me so much, I lost so much confidence. I was so embarrassed that I got treated like this—what was so wrong with me? I never wanted anyone to know I was bullied, I was so ashamed. It took me years to realise there was nothing wrong with me, that these girls just saw the vulnerability in me. If only I knew that bullies are people that are hurting within themselves. Someone in their life is hurting/bullying them in some way. If anyone is bullying you just say to them: I feel sorry for you, you must be a sad person, hurting inside. They will most likely back off when you say that.

As previously mentioned to go with one of my goals, I did a small story of who I am, with photos of who is important to me, like my family, my friends and books. This reminds me of all the attributes that I am working on, and if I find myself lacking any of these, I look at it and read it out loud until I believe it to be true.

Don't get me wrong, there are still days where I feel as though I am struggling, and I look at this at think, "What am I on about?" This is my subconscious not being used to me thinking these positive thoughts about myself, and I have to remind myself that I am human and there are times that I feel down, and this is okay. It's not okay to keep myself in this deep dark feeling for too long because that is where all the negative thoughts begin to surface again.

At work one day in 2020, I was beginning to feel a little bit down.

We had a 'thank you' box for us teachers to write in and thank each other for something.

Well, I wrote, "Thank you to myself for being so amazing. I love every-one". At the time this helped, and when I had to read out the message I did feel a little bit silly! Everyone did laugh though, so this was good.

It is important to write and say nice things about yourself—especially when you're feeling down. You need to believe in yourself and give yourself credit. You are doing the best you know how to.

We are all humans, and we all make mistakes. If we are learning from our mistakes, this is all that matters, and that we are accountable to them. But sometimes, we put so much pressure and doubt on ourselves. These thoughts don't come from other people, we wouldn't let other people talk to us that way, so why do we allow ourselves?

You can be or change anything in your life that you want! Your behaviour causes your results. Basically, you can be anything you want to, you just have to believe you can do it.

Give yourself permission to say no to your family or friends without feeling guilty. You cannot do everything all the time for everyone. Some of you may already do this, and for some this will be really hard!

I had to work really hard on this and be sure I practiced saying no. The more said no, the easier it became. And those I was saying no to were really understanding. Sometimes you have to think, "Who am I doing this thing for?" And if it doesn't add value to you, why are you doing it?

Make a choice to forgive not only others in your life, but most importantly yourself. Free yourself from anger and resentment towards past events you cannot control and people you can't change. The only thing you can change is yourself and the way you respond to situations out of your control.

Allow yourself to not feel guilty about the past. The past has been and gone, it cannot be changed. Accept what has been, and find it in you to forgive and let go. Once you forgive and let go, you will begin the journey to wellbeing, and you will begin to heal.

Connect with yourself, allow yourself the time to be fully present. To be fully present is to be still. Ideally, you could be out in nature, at the beach or river, or at a park. Just sit still. And listen. Listen to the birds, the wind blowing. Look around and watch the leaves, or flowers. Or close your eyes and listen if you wish. Try not to think. Every time you think a thought, let it go and just try to clear your head of thoughts. It's a really hard thing to do, but keep practicing. Allow yourself the time and space to keep trying. I suggest you start off with at least fifteen– twenty minutes of just practicing being present each week.

Being fully present means you aren't thinking or worrying about anything. The world outside of where you are does not exist, even if it's for a short while.

Try not to be anxious about the future. The future has not arrived yet, and pre-empting what could or might happen will only worry you with negative energy—not to mention it can cause unnecessary sickness.

Often, when the time comes that I was so worried about, it isn't as bad as I thought it would be!

I know it's easier said than done, but if you do find yourself worrying or imagining something that may happen, change the thought. Replace it with a positive thought—retrain your mind. This takes time, so go easy on yourself, look after yourself and be gentle. Think to yourself, where would you be without that thought? How would you feel without that thought? Allow yourself the confidence to SHINE! Only YOU can get yourself unstuck—you are in control of YOU!

Knowing the storm will pass

Like I have said earlier, storms come and go. Some storms last longer than others, some change direction when we least expect it, and some resurface when we think they've finished, leaving us feeling stuck!

This is what happened to me. I thought a storm I was facing had come to an end, but it started up again and became even bigger than the storm I'd just faced. I had a choice. We all have choices. I chose to ride with the storm. I felt the emotions, and at times I blamed others. I allowed myself to feel self-pity for a split moment, fell and hit the bottom. I really thought when I got to the bottom, "It's an awful long way back up, and I am not sure if I can get back up there." It was at that moment that, with the help and support of my amazing husband, I decided to pick myself back up and get back to where I belonged. I had to stop blaming others and look at myself, and how I was responding.

I've said earlier that being judged was a fear of mine, and I knew people talked about me. I'm sure right now as you're reading my book you will possibly be judging me and have an opinion of me. This was my ego, and I didn't want people to talk badly of me, but in reality I had to realise that people are going to judge, they are going to have an opinion and they are going to talk about me. I cannot control what others say, feel or do, but what I can control are my feelings and my response.

I began to stop giving my energy to what I thought other people may be thinking or saying, and if I did hear comments of things people had said, I didn't let it worry me. I then realised this storm would pass, and it did. I got back up, and I felt better than I had before. I had learnt so much through that storm. Even though I know there will be another storm at some point in my life, and I may not be fully prepared for it, I know I will learn something from it, and I will rise a stronger person. It's my thoughts and how I respond to the storm that will get me through.

Sometimes you may experience a feeling inside you that you just don't know if you can carry on your life, and this is not a nice feeling to have. You really begin to think you're crazy, and you can't tell anyone that you've had these thoughts. If you've had these thoughts and not followed through with them, you have survived. You are successful at this! If right now you are thinking you have never achieved anything in your life—you have achieved this! You've reached a point in your life where you felt so down that you didn't want your life to continue—yet you are still here! I can only say for myself that I have had these thoughts, and I've thought I was crazy. Why am I thinking these thoughts? What is wrong with me? But something has stopped me from doing anything about it, not to mention these days I would miss my husband, daughters and granddaughter far too much—and I don't want to miss out on milestones in their lives. But there was a time in my life that I didn't have any of these people in my life. At age fifteen I did try to end my life. I was in so much pain, and I wanted that pain to go away. I was a very confused teenager, and I think all I needed was my mum to love and hold me—to tell me she loved me.

How you feel today is not necessarily how you may feel in a year. The storm you went through last year will become a different storm next year.

Finding out how you can survive your storms will be your success. In life there will be many different storms. You'll go through so many different moments, some good, and some not so good, but in every chapter of you life you can learn from the storms. There are lessons in everything we do, and if we are present enough and tuned in, sometimes we can understand the lesson. But if we do not understand the lesson, the storm may continue to keep coming back in different ways to try to teach us. If you do ever get to such a bad place that you are close to ending your life, I would highly recommend talking to a counsellor or someone that you trust. You don't need to tell your friend what is in your thoughts, just make sure you have someone with you encouraging and helping you through your struggles. At the end of this book I will also leave my contact details, so if you wish to you can get in contact with me.

Showing up – looking in the mirror

Sarah asked me, how did I show up? How did I want to show up? I used to wear hoodies and track pants to work all the time and only dress up if I was going to a meeting. How did this show how I valued myself? I had never thought of it from this perspective. So the first thing I changed was what I wore. I put a little bit of make up on every day and worked on how I was showing up. I began to feel great, and I actually began showing up. I received comments about how great I looked, and I really began to feel and act great!

One of the phone calls I had with Sarah had me in tears. She asked me to look in the mirror. The reason these things were happening was my fault, and I was responsible. At the time I was so emotional, I remember thinking back to when I was a child and my mum had told me how I was feeling. I felt so angry at how Sarah was telling me how I felt. I became defensive and didn't want to hear what she had to say. However, after I had the time to reflect and go back to what she was saying, Sarah wasn't fully blaming me, she just said I was responsible for how I responded. Looking in the mirror to who do you want to be, how are you showing up? How do you want to show up? I certainly know now that wearing just a small amount of make up and tidy clothes helps me show up and act the way I want to act. It's really interesting how making such a small change in what you wear can help you to feel different or show up better. What colour do you wear that makes you feel happy? Or do you have a colour that people say looks really good on you?

Listen to the language you use on a daily basis. Are you a positive person? Is the language you use positive or negative? Do you gossip? Do you use words like, "I'll try, do you swear a lot? (angry people swear) I should, I could, I might?". Listen to yourself. Catch your thoughts and turn them around to, "I will, I can." Cancel negative thoughts or words spoken. Start to see and feel the difference in your life.

When I had my childcare centre, I was ALWAYS busy. I told myself and everyone around me I was always busy. And guess why I was busy? Yep, you guessed right—because I told myself I was busy. I needed to change that thought into a positive one, such as "I am productive." The point I am getting at is you are what you think you are, and you will feel how you think you feel.

I remember Stu telling me he always disliked Mondays. He really struggled with getting out of bed on Mondays and going to work. It wasn't until he thought to himself one day, "Come on Stu, you have to accept Mondays, they come around every week. You can't change them, so you might as well accept it." And from that moment on, he didn't struggle with Mondays anymore.

Talking to someone you have a great relationship with

In all of my years of struggles and storms, I remember only being able to really talk honestly to those who I trusted and had a relationship with. My mum tried to introduce me to counselling, however this felt so strange for me as I didn't connect with the counsellor. Depending on the nature of your struggle, talking to a close friend or partner may help—not always do we need solutions. Sometimes, we just need someone to talk to.

Sometimes, we do need to talk to someone who would be honest with us. This is where talking to Sarah was good as she did say things I didn't want to hear, but if she didn't, what would I have learnt? So really think about what it is you want from who you will talk to, but be prepared. You may not like the feedback that you get, but this is so important in order for you to be able to grow. Often, we talk to those who will not be 100% honest with us, so choose what feedback you want. Do you want honest feedback, or do you just need someone to vent to?

If what you are going through is a serious struggle, you might be in a really bad way, with negative thoughts about harming yourself. I would highly suggest phoning a help line, going to your doctor or someone that you trust. Look for a counsellor to talk to. If you don't connect with the counsellor you go to, try another. If you are spiritual, sometimes a spiritual healer may be able to help. Or if you go to church, possibly you have someone close at church you could talk to. There will always be someone or somewhere to turn for help. PLEASE don't stay inside your own head with your negative thoughts.

During Covid-19, I became close to one of my good friends who also owns a childcare centre, and we share similar stories. It was really helpful talking to her. She was empathetic as she had been through what I was going through, and she really understood how I was feeling. Sometimes, talking to someone that has been through similar situations as you can be really helpful.

Talking to someone you trust can be hard, and you may feel as though you will be judged. But trust me, if you are judged for speaking your truth, find someone else to talk to! Mental health problems, depression any times you feel down is hard to deal with, and you do not need to go through any of it alone. And you should not go through it alone! Always think, "How I am feeling today is not how you will always feel!" In a years' time from now, you will feel differently, and most likely, your storm will have passed. Think of a time that you have been through, a hard time, like a breakup, for instance. Remember the pain you felt and thinking you would never get over the breakup. Do you remember that time helped with the pain? A year or two after your breakup, you began to live your life again. Time does heal. Allow yourself the time to go through the grieving process and the feelings you experience during the hard time and know that you can feel great again!

Talking about how you are feeling, acknowledging how you are feeling or saying these things out loud can sometimes be so hard! However, saying these things and then letting them go is so important. Sometimes, you may now know how you are feeling, so this is where talking to a professional can help you to get in touch with your feelings. There are support groups for various forms of trauma—lots can be found on the internet. As I have said google has become my best friend.

For me, I found it hard to talk about how I had been in foster care as a child and taken away from my mum. It really hurt, and I didn't want to feel the feeling again, but the healing took place the more I spoke about it—and the more I began to understand it. I made sense of it by talking out loud to my friends, and now I don't choke on my words when I remember the feeling of when I was in foster care. I have accepted this is my past. I can't change what happened, or how those teenage years went, but I can still have a voice and share my experiences about it—without it hurting.

Looking at your achievements

Sarah suggested in her book to look at all of your achievements over the past ten years and then write down where you want to be in ten years. What do you want to achieve in the next ten years? Maybe you want to buy a house, change jobs? In your journal, write your lists. You will be actually really surprised at all the things you have achieved!

I wrote down all the things I had achieved in the past ten years, and I was actually super amazed at all the things on the list. I know having my husband has helped me achieve a lot of what I have, however I also know it was through my determination and persistence as well.

We all like to feel proud and good about ourselves, especially when we're feeling down or going through hard times. So writing a list of all our achievements is a really great exercise to do. It's a really inspirational activity to do.

When I wrote down what I would like to achieve in the next ten years, I found a bit of a struggle—especially when I was in a negative, struggling mindset. So you definitely need to do this when you are feeling inspired.

It's natural to dream and to want better for ourselves, so when you're dreaming of what you'd like to achieve in the next ten years, be as specific as you can. For example, if you want to make more money, be specific about how much more money you'll make. In the book "Into the magic shop" James Doty talks about visualizing your dreams and being sure to make sure you actually see yourself with whatever it is you are dreaming about. If you believe you can achieve, you will.

The Last Chapter

♥

"*L* *ife now as we know it"*

Fast forward now to 2022. At forty-one-years old, I had this niggling feeling inside me that I had to make contact with Mr Watson—the teacher I talked about in the "Influences" chapter—who trained me for the finals in the cross country.

All these years I remembered him, and often, I tell people how this teacher believed in me. He spent his own time after school to train me. I felt as though all these years, he had made a real impact on my life. I wanted to get in touch with him and tell him about my life, about this book and the influence he had on me.

So, I set out to search for him! I emailed my old primary school, explaining the story and that I only knew his last name and the colour and make of the car he had driven back in 1990!

A couple of days later, I received a reply! The office lady must have thought, this lady is crazy! Now thirty-years-later, and I still remember his car and the colour! Well, she only had an initial for me. "Hi, Sharon. I found a Mr J Watson in our records who was the deputy principal under Mr Snookes," she suggested I could ask around on a Devonport Facebook page. So that's what I did! Exciting! I thought, what am I going to tell him when he gets in touch with me? Where will I start?

Then there was a comment... Someone remembered "Julian Watson"—he had been a principal at a school in Taumaranui. OH MY GOD! I had lived there too—but earlier than he had! And then another comment: "I remember Julian Watson from my kids' time at Bayswater. I heard he died some years ago." Um.... what? I thought, OH MY GOD! No way! What? Hopefully she heard wrong!

So. I searched Mr Snookes on Facebook, and I sent him a message! I was thinking he probably wouldn't reply, but something inside me thought, just do it anyway. A few days went by, and then came a reply! "Hi, Sharon. Unfortunately Julian Watson passed away some years ago with the dreaded cancer." Well, that's that then!

Often in life, things don't turn out the way you'd like them to. I mean, I knew it had been thirty years, but he wasn't that old thirty years ago, surely? I felt very sad that I never got the chance to thank him for the impact he had on my life as a young girl at Bayswater Primary School or the chance to laugh together about how I had let him down on the day of the run because of my asthma attack!

So thank you, Mr Watson. R.I.P—till we meet again someday... If any of his family do ever read this book, I hope you find comfort in reading my tribute to Mr Watson. He really was the kindest teacher, he believed in me. Something I will hold close to me forever.

My takeaway from this is to live each day to the fullest. If you find yourself thinking about someone from your past or present, get in touch with them. Let them know you are thinking about them, and make sure they know what you would want them to know. Because you might find yourself in my situation, and it might be too late. I heard this quote the other day: "Now is good."

As I sit and think about my life, where I have travelled and where I am today, I reflect on all those emotions and thoughts going through my head.

Writing this book has been a great healing process for me; it has also opened up a whole new me. A few months ago—maybe even a year ago—I had this crazy thought! Yup, you guessed it... Another crazy thought! I thought I might be ready to meet my biological father! I tossed around the idea with my husband and a few of my really close friends. My husband was super supportive, as he always is. He warned me if I went through with meeting James, that this will bring up all sorts of triggers and emotions for me and to be prepared.

I left it for a few months, then I revisited it. I thought to myself If I was going to do this, I would have to be careful. I had to be sure I wouldn't open up a whole can of worms. There were my girls to think about and my mum—I have always felt I have needed to protect her. What would she think? What if me contacting him gave him the idea to visit my mum again?

So many things were running through my head! I then spoke to my dad about the idea, not to get his approval but just out of respect, and I wanted him to know I was happy with him as my dad. I wasn't replacing him. He was also really supportive and said just to be careful. More time went on, and I still found myself unsure.

I spoke to a friend of ours who is a retired detective and whom I have a huge amount of respect for. I asked him what he thought. His words were, "If you don't do it, you will always wonder, and you may have regrets. You won't know until you try."

A few more months went by. I spoke to Mum about how me contacting my biological father would affect her and I needed to protect her. Mum was supportive also. She did ask if I would go to counselling first to make sure it was the right thing for me. I explained to her that I was just thinking about it at this stage and would not be making the decision lightly. There is so much to think about; I have three children that I also need to protect.

A few months later, I met a lovely author while we were camping over the summer holiday. She had some aspirational cards she asked me to shuffle. The card I received was "Forgiveness". She said I needed to forgive someone, though it didn't need to be to them directly but within myself.

Was this my father James she was talking about?

A few more months went by, and then I made the decision I would contact him! I set up a Facebook account and messaged him, saying I thought I was ready to meet. However, I needed him to promise me he would not try to contact my mum at all. I waited anxiously for his reply, checking back every so often to see if he had replied.

A few hours later, HE REPLIED! He promised he would not contact my mother. So I asked for his phone number and told him I would phone him the next day, as it was quite late. He told me he was on his boat as he lived on Great Barrier Island, and that it was super rough with the cyclone! OH MY GOD! I could not believe what I had just done! I asked my cousin (his niece) to phone me, and I told her what I had done!

My cousin and I have always been close, and I have a huge respect for her. We had a great conversation. She then also told me a close family member of ours had moved down this way! Um, what? What had I just heard? Wow, all this information was all so crazy!

I remember thinking, oh my god. What if something happened to him on his boat and I didn't get the chance to meet him? What if he wasn't on a boat at all and he made it up? And what if he drove down to my hometown to find my mum? What if it was someone pretending to be him, and it wasn't him at all? So many crazy thoughts were going through my head. I needed to sleep! But my mind was racing, and my heart was racing even faster.

My body felt strange. I didn't know what I was feeling. What had just happened? Back to my heart racing again, then the questioning thoughts—What am I feeling? I can't sleep... Should I get up and do some work? Write in my book? And then I must have eventually drifted off to sleep, because the next thing I woke up.

Heart racing again! This went on for days, my heart racing! I decided to message one of family members, thoughts were racing through my head again. What if they didn't want to talk to me? What if they were angry at me for contacting them and James? They messaged me back! And OH MY GOD again! I felt like all this was just a dream, a movie, not real and this was not happening! They live in a similar area to my mum! I felt like a little child replying, then anxiously waiting for a reply back... Then came a reply! We shared a few messages back and forth.

Whenever I feel like my mind is clogged up with information, I find that running or exercising is great for me. So I went to the gym, then phoned him! My heart was racing again, my body tensing up, I remember dialing the number, double checking if I had the number right. My hands were sweating and shaking. I could feel the blood running through my veins... It rang a few times, then he answered. "Hello."... Shit, now what do I say? I didn't have a script!

"Hi, this is Sharon," I said.

"Who?" he replied.

OH MY GOD, are you serious? I was thinking. Did he forget I was phoning?

"Sharon," I replied.

And he said, "Argh, yes, sorry. My boat has gone on its side, and I don't know what to do."

So I told him I will call him back later, and he says, "Thank you, Sharon," and that was that! Conversation over!

It was windy, and I could hear the wind blowing in the background. But this guy did not sound like I had expected him to sound. I mean, what did I actually expect him to sound like! What had I imagined him to sound like? He sounded so young! Like a friend of mine would sound... Was it actually James I was talking to, or was this a setup? So many things were now going through my mind. My mind was going a hundred miles an hour. Get it together, Sharon!

I went for my run on the cross trainer. Then when I got home, I phoned my mum to tell her the news. I didn't want her bumping into my family in her hometown and freaking out! But I also realise I cannot protect her.

She took it as I expected, but at the same time, she was strong. She asked me if he was married, would I let my girls meet him, and how did he get the money to buy a boat. She was not listening to me! I had told her we spoke on the phone for like two seconds! I do not know how I would have got all that information from him in that short phone call! So I again repeated myself and said it was a very quick two-second phone call.

I told her I get it, I understand her fear, but I said to her maybe she needs to face her fear too. She warned me that he may just turn up at my house one day, uninvited, and she hoped I was prepared for what could happen.

I spoke a lot about my feelings and what was going on in my head with Stu and a very good friend of mine, going through the scenarios and what-ifs. These conversations helped me to cope. I also found going for long walks or runs outside in the fresh air really helped with my mental health.

At this stage, I planned to be in control, I would meet or talk with him on my terms and my terms only.

You see, I get it, I get the things that he has done and how frightened my mother is of him, but I do not want to live in this fear anymore. I am not going to. I have a dad, I don't need a dad. I love my dad. I just want some answers and I want closure. I don't want to go to bed at night wondering if he will turn up.

In all honesty, he has not turned up since I was eighteen—that was twenty-two years ago! Is he really going to now? Maybe he will, maybe he won't.

Maybe me contacting him will open a can of worms, maybe it won't.

If I live my life not taking risks or stepping outside of my comfort zone, how will I ever get anywhere? And I do not want to be in the same place in life, year after year. Everything we do in life is a risk. I mean, driving down to the shop to buy some milk is a risk! Changing houses or jobs is a risk. So if you think deeply, almost everything we do in life is a risk! Writing this book is a risk, a risk people will read it and get angry at me, or they will love it and will relate, or a risk that it will be boring. But it's the risk I want to take.

Just like the risk of contacting James, right now. I don't know how this is going to turn out. I don't know if he is going to turn up at my house one day. And if he does, what will I do? I do know that I still think the same way though—that one day he could turn up at my house even if I didn't contact him! As you can see, I am a normal human being, just like you! I think lots of thoughts, but I know these are thoughts and feelings that I am going through are only part of the present moment. Tomorrow will be another day, and I will be faced with something different.

So the whole day passed, but the weather did not improve, and I decided not to phone James back. I did check the Facebook account I had set up in case he had messaged me. But no... there were no messages. What was I expecting anyway? Him to message me and say, "Is now is a good time to call?"

Now the feeling of being sick in my stomach was beginning to come back. Why did I care so much and why was I feeling like this? What about

James, how was he feeling? Did I stop and think about that? This moment in his life he probably gave up on a long time ago—his daughter making contact with him! What was going through his mind? Had I triggered something in him? This, I am sure, would have brought up a whole lot of emotions and memories for him. I think it is at this point that I truly feel at peace with what has happened in my life.

I know my mum has told me about things that he did, and I saw some of these things myself. I also saw and witnessed some crazy things my mum did at times. My mum was an alcoholic; she is now a recovering alcoholic. She made the choice to put herself into rehab, for whatever reason she had. Yes, I am proud of my mum for not drinking for—I think—ten years. But this has not changed the demons she has inside her. It does not change her outbursts that she has randomly and with no warning at all. So my mum was definitely no saint, just like James wasn't either.

The difference is that I grew up with my mother, knowing what she was capable of doing. I did not grow up with James and had no idea idea what he is capable of—and still don't. Yes, often I am hard on my mum, and today, when she assumed so many things about James, I got frustrated with her. I felt myself breathing fast, my fists beginning to tense up. I went straight to defence mode. And before I knew it, I heard myself defending this guy I don't even know! But on the other hand, when people talk about my mum in a similar way, I too find myself defending her. I find the good in what she has done.

And although I do not know the good in what James has done, I think, he is still a human, he must have feelings, and I am sure somewhere he would have empathy. And if he doesn't have empathy, well, I am about to find this out—as he may turn up at my house! You see, I could keep on going around in round in circles, tormenting my mind with all the thoughts and scenarios... And what good is all this going to do for me?

All the scenarios are not going to happen! Maybe not even any of these fears will happen. And all I am doing to myself is wasting my time and my day, worrying about something that is probably not going to happen! And if it does happen, I can't change anything. I am not in control of how others respond or what they do or don't do. I am only in charge of what I do, how I feel and how I respond. This theory seems easy when you write it down, especially when I feel like I am giving someone else this advice, but it's harder to follow for yourself.

Have you ever been in a situation where you have given advice so easily and then you have gone through the exact same scenario, but yet when you go through it your whole world is turning upside down? Yep, we are all so great at giving out advice to others but struggle to either give ourselves the advice or to take it from others. This is because our brain listens to what we tell it, and often we think negative thoughts about ourselves.

A few days after I first phoned James, I still had not phoned him back! I wasn't sure if I should phone him, I had got inside my head and was doubting if I should now. I was beginning to think, oh my god, what will I say?

A few days later, I logged into Facebook to find a message from James, saying it was nice to hear from me the other day and that I could phone him when I was free! So I did!

We talked, and I told him a little bit about myself and what I had been up to. He told me about where he was living. I then told him I had been afraid of him as a child, and I still was—then I started to cry. I was not telling him that for him to feel bad—I needed to tell him how I felt. This is part of my healing. And I really felt so much better just saying it out loud to him! He did, of course, feel bad and said, "Oh no, you shouldn't feel like that."

We continued talking. I asked him how long had he been clean for. He said over ten years, which was great.

He had told me he had been in CYF (Child, Youth and Family) care as a child also, and he was beaten up in the home. I told him of my interest in psychology, the brain, and how important the first 1000 days are. So many years have been lost.

He said the last time he saw me, I was just eleven, he thought. And yes, that was kind of true—that was the last time we spoke together. When I was eleven, I did visit him in jail a few times. I didn't like going to the jail, and it never felt right so I stopped going. I reminded him of the time he came to Palmy when I was eighteen, but he did not want to be reminded of that. We ran out of conversation, and I had to go cook dinner anyway.

He told me he loved me, and we said goodbye. Wow, after all these years, I have faced my fear! I have contacted the man I called "Daddy" as a young girl! I really feel like this was the right thing to do, and I truly believe he does not want to cause me any harm. I have not spoken to my mum about our second phone call, as I don't think I need to concern her with the details of the call.

So, where to from here? Well, I have not messaged him nor have I heard from him. I do feel like he probably has a whole lot of emotions going on inside of him that he has to process and deal with. Maybe I will leave it for a while and then message him, seeing how he is doing. I would be interested to know what he is feeling and thinking. And then I guess at some point later in the year, it would be great to meet him and have a memory of him outside of prison.

A few days later, I plucked up the courage to message him. I asked him how he was and hoped I hadn't brought up a whole lot of emotions for him. On his reply, I asked if we should meet up and that I really wanted a memory of meeting my bio father outside of prison. We have arranged to meet up on his BIRTHDAY! I asked him what café or restaurant shall we go to and... His response was, let's go through the drive through of KFC and then go sit on the beach!

James, I know you are reading this and by now, we would have met, and I mean no disrespect to you at all, but KFC on the beach!? At first, I thought, oh my god, and I was a little nervous about the beach. I was thinking somewhere more a little public. (I have trust issues remember). But Stu said the beach would be really nice, provided it was a nice day!

So... we were a week out till we headed up to Auckland to meet James! My husband had not long had Covid, so we all had to isolate for seven days! Luckily or not so lucky, I didn't get it! So, all going well, the plan was still to be going to Auckland—provided me or my daughter doesn't get the dreaded Covid! I think if that does happen, I will not be wanting to go another time. I have worked myself up so much for this meeting and am not sure I could or want to go through all this again!

In my mind, I have already had to change the date that we were originally going to meet him, so I think if we have to change it again, I will just cancel it altogether. I have hyped myself so much for this to happen that if it doesn't, then I will be okay with that. I am okay with just having talked to him on the phone and knowing that I have put closure to my past, that I no longer live in fear of waking up to James being at my window or turning up to my house or my mum's house.

For all these years, I have felt responsible for protecting my mum—but I can let it go and be at peace. If I do get to meet James, I am nervous. I don't know what to expect. I can only imagine what he will look like, what it will be like when I first see him, how will it be, what conversations will we have... What will Stu think of him? What will be going through James's mind and what will he be feeling? Stu tells me he will be feeling all sorts of emotions too, and yes, I know he will be.

Well, the day before I am about to meet James. I remember feeling so nervous, I couldn't breathe very well. So many thoughts were going through my mind. I knew I needed to calm down and just let what will be, be. Sitting there all alone at my sister-in-law's, I felt so abandoned. Stu had gone out with his sister. I thought I would be okay on my own, but it turned out, I was not! What if James doesn't turn up? What if he is really scary looking and I wish I hadn't contacted him?

It's been thirty years since I have seen my birth father, and when I did see him, he was in jail! It really was not a nice place for an eleven-year-old to go. I only went a couple of times, as I did not like the environment. So mostly, the reason I want this meeting is so I can face the fear I have had most of my life of my birth father and to meet him outside of jail. I have so many questions and memories that I want clarified, so hopefully James will be able to answer these for me.

The next day, when I woke up, I remember thinking, "What am I doing? Am I really going to meet my birth father today?" I had a shower and some breakfast, although I really did not feel like eating! And then we headed off to Auckland. I couldn't breathe, my chest was tight. I was feeling so anxious! It was the quietest trip to Auckland!

On the way there, my aunty messaged me saying she was thinking of me and said that James had messaged her too, saying he was a nervous wreck. I could have easily decided not to go through with this meeting. I really felt so scared and nervous. I felt like no one really understood how I was feeling. This was a HUGE deal! But... I know I have felt like this before, and I have always gone through with the hard decisions or things in my life, and they had turned out okay. I had come this far, I wasn't going to change my mind, not now. And I knew that tomorrow or the next day, I would feel okay again, and this feeling inside me was just going to be short lived. I just had to keep reminding myself that once again, I am so very grateful for my amazing husband. Boy, he has put up with a lot from me over the last seventeen years!

When we arrived in Auckland at our destination, I messaged James to tell him where to meet us. Stu and I sat on the park bench, and my nerves were getting stronger and stronger. Stu said, "I think this must be him walking down." I couldn't look, I didn't want to turn and look.

Oh my god should we just go? What is he going to be like? Sharon, pull yourself together, you have got this! I thought to myself. You are resilient and strong. Just think about how you will feel after this is all over. I felt so much like I was in a movie. I stood up, nervously, turned and looked him. It was him. I began to walk towards him, looking at him for the first time in thirty years, and this time I was not visiting him in jail. He had tears in his eyes and gave me a hug. He looked very well dressed with what looked like a new shirt. Stu introduced himself and shook his hand. As we started to talk, I had my hands on my hips, and I noticed James did too! We were both standing similar!

We walked down closer to the beach, in the nice sunshine and sat on a park bench. I could see us sitting there. I felt like I was looking down at myself, like I was watching myself on the tv program called "Missing Pieces". Missing Pieces is a program where people go in search of family members they have lost or never met. They often meet up on the beach. It was such a surreal feeling, I actually don't know how I was feeling. I couldn't talk, I was at a loss for words. I didn't know what to say! I am so grateful for Stu, as he made conversation when there was silence. This happened a lot! James mentioned that he had watched Missing Pieces and he had thought about going on it to find me. Oh my god, he knew what I was thinking!

I found out I could possibly have a brother! My mum had mentioned this to me over the years, but nothing had ever come of it. James said he had got a phone call saying he was a father. The baby got adopted out, and I think that was that. He didn't really go into great detail about it. And it doesn't matter, I don't need another brother.

James said he had given up hope of ever seeing me again. He had gone to court to try and see me for a Christmas, but the judge said, "Not this Christmas, possibly next Christmas." Nothing really came of that either!

We went up to the restaurant for lunch and continued our conversations. I was feeling really strange and so nervous. I actually don't know what I was feeling or what I was thinking. I felt numb. I felt similar to how I had felt when I first met him when I was eleven. I struggled to make conversation, I had no idea what to say to him. Stu said James kept looking at me and was mesmerized by me. I looked in his eyes a couple of times, and they reminded me of when I was little. I definitely knew that I was connected to this man, it is hard to explain but I guess I had remembered him being my dad... Then I remembered that he had half of a thumb or finger or something. And yep, he showed me! He told me that when he was in my life, he didn't want to spoil me, and that my papa would offer me lollies, and he would say, "No, we are not spoiling Sharon."

I asked him about the time he had picked me up and told my mum he would take me and she would never see me again. He said he didn't really remember, and I could see it was hard for him to talk about some of the things that had happened in his past. I know this as when he mentioned when he was in jail, he referred to it as "that place". And you could see in his eyes that it hurt him to talk about it. He told me he had lots to tell me, but unless I really needed to know, he would not tell me as it did hurt a lot.

So I did it! I faced my fear! How did I do that, you are probably wondering. With believing in myself. Setting that goal. Talking with my husband and a few of my friends. I did some journalling on how I was feeling and what I was thinking. And I remained focused and positive.

I know I have support around me, and I am in a really good place now. Stu had warned me that this could trigger emotions of my past. And I was well aware that this could be the case. So talking and allowing myself to feel the emotions would be really important.

I found journaling really helpful, writing down how I was feeling and was going on for me. Reading a lot of self help books that I could connect with also helped. I also found it helpful to use little affirmation cards, picking one out each day, reading what it said and believing in myself.

If you have hard events coming up in your lives that you are anxious about, my advice to you is to talk about your feelings with your friends or family, or even a professional. If you can't talk about it, write down how you are feeling.

What an amazing feeling! For all my life, I have held on to all these thoughts and emotion and now I'm finally able to have closure and put it in the past. You see, I am a big believer in the past staying in the past—I think we all need to deal with our past at some time in our lives, and in order to live in the present, we shouldn't be distracted with the past or the future.

You can't change what has happened in the past, it has been and gone. You can learn and grow from your past, and I believe the past helps shape the person you are right now in the present. The future has not been yet. I don't know about you, but I often worry about something that hasn't happened yet—it may not even happen, and worrying about the future is also distracting you from being in the present moment.

The past is history.

The future is a mistery.

The present is a gift.

Conclusion

♥

"*In the end, be proud of your journey*"

Trauma effects each of us differently, however any form of trauma has a massive impact on the brain. Research does show that you can heal the brain and rewire its connections. And for me, with the trauma of my upbringing, I found the beginning really hard. Whenever I thought about being in foster care, or spoke about this, I would break down in tears, and the hurt was very raw. But with time and being able to talk about the experiences and feel the emotions, I am now able to freely talk about these experiences and not cry or feel the hurt that I once felt. I found that talking to my close friends about my experiences helped. If I met a new friend, I wouldn't talk to them about my experiences. At times, conversations may have come up where it was appropriate to mention small snippets of my childhood experiences. For years, I was ashamed that I had a baby at sixteen-years-old. Stu has helped me own my past, be proud of who I am and most certainly helped me with the person I have become.

Holding on to experiences or past events cannot be a good thing, this certainly can eat you up. While you are reliving your past, you are not fully present in the moment of now. What happened in the past cannot be changed, what happened yesterday has gone. It's what you do today that's important. But I do think you need to find some way to accept your past, accept the trauma or experiences that happened. It's unfortunate that anyone goes through trauma, especially in their early childhood years. Nothing can take away what happened. If you can find the strength, I would advise you to seek professional advice and work with them to break the cycle. Break the cycle, so you don't have to put your children through similar trauma.

Only you can make the changes you may need to make to create a better future for yourself. And that can start today! Anyone can make changes, you can be anything you want to be. Start making the change today! And my first piece of advice would be to find a way to be at peace with your past and forgive yourself or others that may need to be forgiven. Remember, people only do what they have learnt to do, and what I mean by that is, you learn from the environment that you grew up in. If the environment is a challenge or not so good—unfortunately, statistics show that history will repeat itself. But at some point the cycle can be broken! I am proof of this! If someone like me can pull myself out of a challenging environment and create a stable and encouraging life, then you can too! If you get stuck and need assistance, I would love to hear your story and see if there is any way I can help. Or if you've also created your own positive life to be proud of, get in touch with me via email.

Three years ago when I set off on the journey to write a book about my life and tools that helped me through dark times, I had a different vision and outlook on my upbringing, my life and the experiences I was given. I began writing this book not knowing my birth father. All I knew about him was what I remembered as a three-year-old, and then watching him on the news when I was ten years old. The only memories I had of him were not good ones, and that was the only information about him I really had to go by. Towards the end of writing this book, I met James. This decision took me a year to make, it was not an easy decision. When I first decided to meet him, I had said to myself, I only wanted to meet him for closure, and that I would not pursue a relationship with him. We have completely different lives. However, after meeting him, I have recently spoken on the phone to him a few times, and I am considering writing a book from his perspective about his life and experiences.

During this time, I also began healing my relationship with my mum. I now have a better understanding of her and what her upbringing was like, and the brain development around her trauma. My mum struggles with me. She struggles to understand me, and I too struggle to understand her. We both have completely different views on life, and this is fine, but we both want to be right. I am concerned my mum lives too much in her past—and don't get me wrong, she did have a rough upbringing—but I wish she would find peace and lock away her past so she can be fully present in the moment, in the now. I know and understand she's suffered from so much trauma in her childhood. My wish for her is that she can find herself in a place where she's at peace with her childhood, so she can enjoy the life she has now and rewrite her script into a positive, happy story.

We are all humans. We all have emotions and feelings, and we all make mistakes. Some of us keep making the same mistakes, but changes can still happen—it's never too late! Mistakes are just lessons we need to learn. Look for failures as opportunities and setback as motivators. Remain positive—trust the process! Life isn't happening to you, life is responding to you.

The past and the memories of what we went through can be so hurtful. Blame can also hurt us, but it doesn't hurt the person we are blaming as in most cases they have no idea we're doing it. Where you can, find a way to be at peace with your past. Accept that has happened in the past, the past has happened, you cannot ever change it. You can only change the present.

I know I've said this before, but forgive those who you need to forgive. If you can't forgive them in person, meditate, or write a forgiveness letter for yourself. Even if you write the letter, and then burn it, saying to yourself "I release the past energy, it no longer serves purpose to me". Most of all, forgive yourself. Give yourself love, nurture, care and all the attention you deserve. You only get one shot at life, and life is too short to be bitter or judgmental to ourself or others.

Surround yourself with people who inspire you, encourage you and believe in you. In the end, you are the only one who can make these changes. So what are you waiting for? Start today. Get in touch with me if you are not sure where to begin, I am always here.

Remind yourself every day that—I am lovable, just as I am. I know love. I can do it, I do it. Positivity is a choice. And finally, I am grateful for every single day of my life! Arohanui. Take care, and all the very best for your journey to wellbeing. I believe we all have resiliency in us, some of us are just stronger and more resilient than others. I know that if you were given a situation where you had to survive, you would show your resiliency and you would survive! It's amazing what we as humans are capable of when we really have to survive.

I wish you all the best and positive vibes as you embark on your healing journey.

Website and Book Recommendations

♥

Brene Brown, author of "Dare to Lead. Living Into Your Values"
Dare to Lead | List of Values - Brené Brown (brenebrown.com)
Jim Doty, author of "Into The Magic Shop"
Into the Magic Shop: The Alphabet of the Heart — The Innerwork Center

Rhonda Byrne, author of "The Secret to Love, Health and Money"
Raewyn Weller, author of "Your HEALTH is your GREATEST WEALTH"
Byron Katie, author of "Loving What Is"
Stephan R Covey, author of "The 7 Habits of Highly Effective People"
Bruce Perry and **Oprah Winfrey,** authors of "What Happened to you?"
Website on Tapa whā,
Māori health models – Te Whare Tapa Whā | Ministry of Health NZ
DR Carol S. Dwek, author of "Mindset"
Louise Hay, author of "You Can Heal Your Life"

Dr Sarah Woodhouse, author of "You're not broken"

Debbie Ford, author of "The Dark Side of the Light Chasers"

Lisa K. PhD, author of "Intuition on Demand"

Mark Manson, author of "The Subtle Art of Not Giving a F*CK"

Nathan Wallis, Neuroscience Educator

Phone numbers for support

Lifeline: 0800 543 354

Youthline: 0800 376 633, or you can text them at 234.

Suicide Crisis Helpline: 0508 828 685

Parent Help: 0800 568 856

Anxiety NZ: 0800 269 4389

Alcohol & Drug Helpline: 0800 787 787

Anxiety NZ: 0800 269 4389

The quotes in each chapter are quotes I have written.

Vision I Created

♥

B elow is the vision I created for the person I want to be today.

I am calm, confident and enthusiastic. I am approachable, honest, clear and respectful. I have a fantastic work life balance. Working with amazing people. My relationship with my husband is strong fun and healthy.
I am healthy and fit, I go to the gym everyday before work and I feel fantastic every day.
I am a great Mum and wife and have quality time with my family every day.
I meet with great friends who inspire me at least once a fortnight, or message them regularly.
I read personal growth books to constantly be learning.

family

live your dream.